Order ID: 203-1507987-9705169

Thank you for buying from june5469 on Amazon Marketplace.

Delivery address:
Tina Townsend Greaves
15 Victoria Street
Clifton
Brighouse
West Yorkshire
HD6 1QS
United Kingdom

Order Date:	21 Nov 2008
Shipping Service:	Standard
Buyer Name:	T J TOWNSEND-GREAVES
Seller Name:	june5469

Quantity	Product Details
1	**Embroiderer's and Quilter's Sourcebook: 1000 Textile Images [Paperback] by...**
	Merchant SKU: F9-KCCC-V2S9
	ASIN: 0713489537
	Order-Item ID: 64577354180083
	Condition: Used - Like New
	Comments: never been used

Thanks for buying on Amazon Marketplace. To provide feedback for the seller please visit
www.amazon.co.uk/feedback. To contact the seller, please visit Amazon.co.uk and click on "Your Account" at the top of
any page. In Your Account, go to the "Where's My Stuff" section and click on the link "Leave seller feedback". Select the
order or click on the "View Order" button. Click on the "seller profile" under the appropriate product. On the lower right
side of the page under "Seller Help", click on "Contact this seller".

EMBROIDERER'S AND QUILTER'S
SOURCEBOOK

EMBROIDERER'S AND QUILTER'S
SOURCEBOOK

ANGELA THOMPSON

First published 2005

Copyright © Angela Thompson 2005

The right of Angela Thompson to be identified as Author of this work has been asserted by her in accordance with the Copyright, Designs and Patents Act 1988.

ISBN 0 7134 8953 7

A CIP catalogue record for this book is available from the British Library.

Printed in China by SNP Leefung
for the publishers:

B T Batsford
Chrysalis Books Group
The Chrysalis Building
Bramley Road
London W10 6SP
www.chrysalisbooks.co.uk

An imprint of Chrysalis Books Group plc

Distributed in the United States and Canada by Sterling Publishing Co., 387 Park Avenue South, New York, NY 10016, USA

CONTENTS

INTRODUCTION

This comprehensive book is intended as a reference source for both the recreational embroiderer and the textile student. At the same time, it is hoped that the wealth of illustrations will inspire embroiderers and quilters to try out new ideas and adapt designs and patterns from the past for their own particular type of craft work.

The development of the historic embroideries illustrated, which can be traced throughout the centuries, ends with their interpretation in the modern idiom and many of our contemporary textile artists have contributed examples of their work. Embroidery techniques of European origin are contrasted with those from other countries and the widely differing world regions. It is hoped that this will inspire the leisure embroiderer and quilter to visit other lands, meet like-minded people and share their stitchery expertise. It is also designed for textile students, to give an illustrated background to the history of embroidery from all over the world.

The greater part of the book is based on the collection of worldwide textiles, gathered together by the author over a period of many years. Victorian embroidery, lace, patchwork, baby-gowns and items of family costume were inherited from a grandmother who never threw anything away. It was this love of embroidery that led to the preservation of embroidery and patchwork made by the author's great grandmother, Matilda Adelaide Bate, as well as that of great, great aunt Jane Bate, an apprentice to a Court Dressmaker who worked for Queen Victoria. These family items became the basis of a collection devoted to different types of stitchery and textile techniques.

The search for new examples led to foreign travel, which in its turn provided an understanding of the methods used by the different craft workers and more importantly, the context in which the textiles are produced. No collection is complete, so the contemporary craft work illustrated in this book, which is not part of the collection, is credited with the name of the individual designer who produced the embroidered or quilted article. Museum collection items are listed under the appropriate headings.

The techniques featured in this guide appear in alphabetical order. Each section is designed to show the development of a particular subject, both through time and across the geographical areas of the world. Dates, which are approximate unless stated otherwise, give a sequence where patterns or methods of working change and develop over a period of time. The individual interpretation of similar stitching techniques used in widely differing communities can be compared, one with another. Some pieces, especially in contemporary work, include a variety of techniques, so these items are catalogued according to the main technique employed. Embroidery stitches are listed in the order of their frequency on each piece, not in their alphabetical order. A guide to the stitches used throughout is available under headings within the Index, which will also give details of the design elements included on the textiles.

Throughout, the measurement of each item illustrated has been included. While this is of great importance to the textile historian, it will also give a sense of scale to the working embroiderer and quilter. The size given is that of the complete item, unless specified otherwise. If the collected item is a fragment of a larger piece, the size of the fragment is given. As the scale of the embroidery shown in the detail illustrations changes, the measurement stated is the exact size of the particular section of the textile shown. In some cases the actual size will be smaller than the illustration, in others, much larger. The measurement of some Museum Collection items is approximate, and should be employed only as a guide.

It is hoped that the embroiderer or quilter who uses this book will gain as much pleasure as the author has in sharing her collection with them.

Angela Thompson, 2005

Chapter One
Appliqué

Hand Appliqué

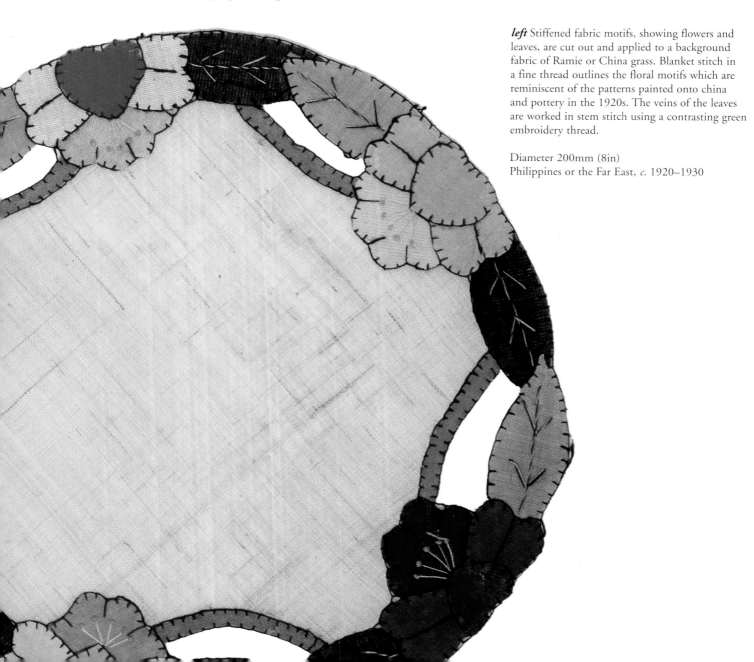

left Stiffened fabric motifs, showing flowers and leaves, are cut out and applied to a background fabric of Ramie or China grass. Blanket stitch in a fine thread outlines the floral motifs which are reminiscent of the patterns painted onto china and pottery in the 1920s. The veins of the leaves are worked in stem stitch using a contrasting green embroidery thread.

Diameter 200mm (8in)
Philippines or the Far East, *c.* 1920–1930

above This slightly transparent, pina cloth tea cosy is made from pineapple leaf fibres. Three hollyhock flowers are worked in blind appliqué, where the raw edges of the coloured fabric are turned under by the needle and sewn in place as the work progresses. Satin, stem and chain stitches form the stalks and leaves, while French knots fill the flower centres.

320 x 250mm (12½ x 9¾in)
Philippines or the Far East, *c.* 1920–1930

right Applied felts and beadwork decorate this charming scene of a Zulu child outside a Kraal circular hut, together with a man drinking from a gourd. A similar combination of hand-stitched felts, string and applied beads, is found on dolls and craft work from the Red Cross Rehabilitation Centre, Durban – a charitable institution.

220–150 x 220mm (8¾–6 x 8¾in)
South Africa, 1950s

above This padded tea cosy, decorated with applied fabrics and hand embroidery stitches, represents a market stall with a woman selling flowers and vegetables to the children. A design typical of the early 1950s, featuring figures in felt appliqué in a whimsical interpretation of Victorian costume.

330 x 220mm (13 x 8¾in)
England, *c.* 1950–1955

above Rilly work is the name given to this type
of applied and quilted patchwork, often used
for bed covers and mats. Squares of seamed
triangles alternate with squares of leaf and flower
patterns. The cut fabric edges are turned under
and hemmed as the work is in progress. The
finished patchwork is quilted to a background
fabric using coarse running stitches in a darker,
contrasting thread.

670 x 840mm (26¼ x 33in)
Sind, Pakistan, *c.* 1970

Three lapel bands from Khon Kaen. Embroidered strips like these are made by Hill-tribe people to apply to the fronts of their indigo-dyed jackets.

top Windmill triangles in alternating red and white fabric are applied to the indigo-printed background.
centre Circular, red pompoms decorate the indigo patterned fabric, alternating with small, red squares of cloth.
bottom Small triangles in folded patchwork are assembled to form squares set within narrow bands of cloth.

70 x 700–800mm (2¾ x 27½–31½in)
North-west Thailand, *c.* 1985

below Both men and women wear versions of this distinctive festival collar. Narrow, overlapping borders of applied fabrics surround squares with double spiral motifs embroidered in cross and stem stiches. The shoulder area spreads out like a small cape and the upstanding collar is stiffened by the consecutive layers of narrow fabric bands.

520 x 200mm (20½ x 8in)
Ghuizhou Province, China, *c.* 1985–1990

below Appliqué pieces featuring landscapes with little padded people were first made as a political statement by women in Chile, whose husbands and sons had suffered under the Pinochet regime. Called *arpilleras* in Chile, they are known as *cuadros* in Peru, where poor women from the shanty towns sell them to earn a living. Satin, stem, blanket and herringbone stitches are used, while a crochet border edges the picture.

200mm sq. (8in sq.)
Lima, Peru, 1986

below This embroidered wall hanging was made by local women in the Johannesburg area. These, together with cushion covers, are sold as a form of income. This picture shows a group of people on their way to Church, bibles in hand, passing a very decorative public convenience. The figures are made with separate arms and feet, giving a three-dimensional effect.

420 x 460mm (16½ x 18in)
South Africa, *c.* 1990

17

Reverse Appliqué

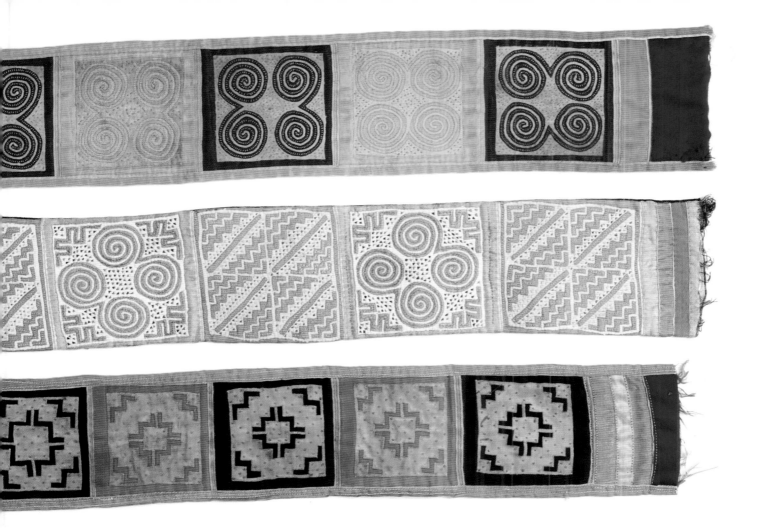

left A petticoat hem is worked in a version
of Carrickmacross lace, where a fabric layer is
placed over a net, the design is embroidered on
top and the surplus fabric is cut away afterwards.
Embroidered as part of her trousseau by Jane
Bate for her wedding to John Hughes in 1861.
The outlines of the little rose flowers are worked
in buttonhole stitch, with the leaf veins in chain
stitch – a labour of love for a very special day.

Detail 175 x 225mm (7 x 9in)
England, 1861
(*Jane Bate*)

above Appliqué and reverse appliqué techniques
are combined with hand embroidery to decorate
these collar bands from northern Laos. They are
examples of fine embroidery from the early 20th
century, worked by the Hmong tribes of the
Golden Triangle.

450–500 x 80mm (17¾–19¾ x 3⅛in)
Northern Laos, 1910–1920

above Traditional cut-paper shapes are the design source for reverse appliqué mats from Hungary and Eastern Europe. The pattern outlines are cut into the top layer of fine, white fabric to reveal the net layer beneath. As the work progresses, the cut fabric edge is stroked under with the needle before sewing down with tiny stitches.

Diameter 230mm (9in)
Hungary, 1950–1960

above Front panel from a Mola blouse, worn by
the Kuna women of the San Blas Islands, off the
Panama coast. The intricate reverse appliqué
technique shows little bird motifs perched within
a cage. Several layers of cloth are used, cut through
to reveal the different colours with the turned
edges held with oversewing stitches.

380 x 250mm (15 x 9⅝in)
San Blas Islands, Panama, *c.* 1970–1975

above The reverse appliqué technique is used for the front panel from a Mola blouse, worn by the Kuna women of the San Blas Islands. In parts of the design, additional colours are inserted beneath the top fabric layer to show a series of rainbow colours. The turned edges of the cut fabric are held with tiny oversewing stitches onto the layer beneath.

350 x 250mm (13¾ x 9⅞in)
San Blas Islands, Panama, 1980s

above Free machine stitching over fabric, cut through various layers of applied fabrics to reveal a background of silk taffeta plaid. This little picture, possibly based on a design from wrought iron, preserves different coloured fabrics in various parts of the motif, which add spontaneity to the overall effect. Unframed, but mounted.

160 x 180mm (6¼ x 7in)
England, 1991
(Lorna Moffat)

Machine Appliqué

above A simple, folded, cut-paper pattern was used for this appliqué mat. Two layers of fabric in contrasting colours are machined together around the design lines and the intervening, surplus fabric cut away. Both the design lines and the raw edges are covered with machine-embroidered satin stitch, angled at the corner points.

230mm sq. (9in sq.)
England, 1978
(Angela Thompson)

right In Hungary, a tradition of embroidery on felt is part of the national heritage. Elaborate designs were worked on the men's white wool coats and today this is echoed in the production of little mats that feature an intricate cutwork pattern applied to a black felt background. The pattern is stamped by machine through the top, red felt layer that is then stitched down onto the black felt ground by sewing machine.

380mm sq. (15in sq.)
Hungary, *c.* 1990

left Machine embroidery both enhances and holds the fabrics and couched cords that form the design area of a small panel supported on natural calico fabric. The background of dyed paper is combined with sheer fabrics and embossed gold to echo the central medallion worked on felt covered with gold embossing powder, heated and imprinted with a fabric stamp.

230 x 160mm (9 x 6¼in)
England, 2004
(Jane Davies)

left Layers of applied fabrics, inspired by Log Cabin Patchwork, are held with both hand and machine embroidery. Some edges are frayed to give a textural quality and small round beads, long bugle beads and decorative sequins are added to give sparkle to the work.

Detail 180 x 150mm (7 x 6in)
England, 2004
(Jane Davies)

right Both hand embroidery and machine-couched yarns form the outer border that frames the central area where strips of fabric are interwoven before applying to the dye-painted background. French knots and crossed stitches in tones of purple, pink and blue contrast with the deep orange and gold of the brown paper base, mounted onto calico fabric before the embroidery is added.

230 x 160mm (9 x 6¼in)
England, 2004
(Jane Davies)

Cutwork

above An Arts and Crafts style peacock is the central feature of this cutwork tea cosy worked on linen crash, mounted over a yellow satin pad. Buttonhole stitches in beige thread outline the cutwork areas of the trellis background. The peacock plume and stylized tail feathers are enhanced with padded satin stitch, while ovals of french knots are worked in a cream silk cord.

390 x 270mm (15¼ x 10½in)
England, *c.* 1910

left A nightdress case in blue linen, embroidered in 'Renaissance cutwork', features little pansy flowers where the leaves and buds are joined with buttonhole bars to form the open spaces of the design. Stem stitch and bullion knots delineate the leaf veins and flower centres and the top flap is bordered with buttonhole scallops, all worked in a white cotton thread.

390 x 200mm (15¼ x 8in)
England, 1950–1960

right A pair of Renaissance work dressing table mats embroidered on white linen in a cutwork technique, popular from the 1930s. A line of running stitch is sewn along the pattern outlines, which are then covered with closely worked buttonhole stitch to give a slightly padded effect to the embroidery. The spaces are cut out after the stitchery is completed.

Diameter 160mm (6¼in)
England, 1930–1950

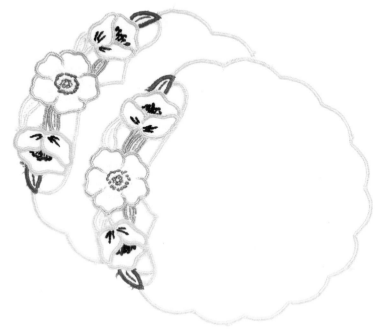

Chapter Two
Beadwork

Europe

below A drawstring bag in cream silk is embroidered with tiny, seed beads. A lazy bead stitch forms beaded loops that define the leaf fronds. The bead strands also form the eight-petalled daisy flowers with their couched beadwork centres. Torchon bobbin lace is added to the front flap and sides of this little Victorian bag, or reticule.

155 x 180mm (6¼ x 7in)
England, *c.* 1840–1850

left A detail of the bead-embroidered front of a little black bag belonging to Matilda Adelaide Bate, the author's great grandmother. Groups of beads are threaded in lazy-stitch fashion to make the leaf fronds and the flower petals that form the central design. A yellow, silk thread is used to stitch the leaf and flower stalks.

Detail 100 x 80mm (4 x 3¼in)
England, *c.* 1840–1850

above A delicate, bead embroidery of tiny, white
flowers forms part of the central garland on this
pale pink pin cushion. The leaf fronds are worked
in groups of strung crystal beads, while a double
row of loops in white and crystal beads forms a
fringe, making it unsuitable for practical use, and
more likely to be a gift for a new-born babe.

200 x 150mm (8 x 6in)
England, *c.* 1845–50

left Small, round beads in white, crystal-grey and black are sewn onto a canvas backing to form a circular design of serrated leaves with stalks and tendrils. Grisaille work, which means grey-coloured, is often combined with cross stitch and red wool in this way. The tent-stitched beads always lie in the opposite direction to the way they are sewn. Possible uses could include a top for a circular box, or a screen to protect the face from an open fire.

Diameter 130mm (5in)
England, *c.* 1850

right Fine beadwork on a circular inset, intended for use as the crown of a baby's bonnet. A scale of 38 threads to the inch (25mm) was used for the design of a rose in the centre of a floral garland, worked in similar sized, round beads onto double-thread canvas. Beads are threaded singly and embroidered as a tent stitch using a finer thread.

Diameter 90mm (3½in)
England, *c.* 1840

left Round, faceted, steel beads are sewn onto the burgundy velvet fabric of a drawstring evening bag. Four-bead clusters are sewn at intervals, while the central grapevine and leaf motif is worked in strands of threaded beads that cover a padding of felt or paper. A trail of cut-steel beads is worked round the border on three sides.

140 x 150mm (5½ x 6in)
England, 1850–1870

right Embroidery on the unfinished top of a circular stool shows the use of tent stitch embroidery in wool, combined with tent stitch sewn beadwork on a double thread canvas. A change of direction in the working of the beads gives modelling to the lily petals, while tones of white and green beads enhance the shading.

Detail 100 x 90mm (4 x 3½in)
England, *c.* 1865–80
(Museum of Costume and Textiles, Nottingham)

left Section of a bolero front, showing tambour beading on a muslin ground, with the addition of floss silk embroidery and including crystal gem stones. The fabric between the beadwork has been cut away by hand. The garment is the product of a professional workshop.

Detail 80 x 110mm (3¼ x 4⅜in)
England or France, *c.* 1890–1900
(Museum of Costume and Textiles, Nottingham)

38

left and below A bead-weaving technique was used to make this evening bag, showing a cartouche containing a spray of flowers. The design is worked by threading beads in the correct order to make each row of the pattern. The fringe is added afterwards by stringing a number of beads, twisting them round and linking through the previous loop.

100 x 140mm (4 x 5½in)
England or France, 1890–1910

left This fragment of a beaded sleeve, made from silk voile mounted over net, is possibly part of a ball gown or presentation dress. The floral motifs are embroidered in silk floss thread using satin stitch, together with faceted steel beads, lapped sequins and seed pearls for the flower centres.

130 x 310mm (5 x 12½in)
England, *c.* 1910
(Museum of Costume and Textiles, Nottingham)

below A panel from an evening dress shows mixed beading methods on voile and net. Silver metallic braids have been sewn to the background, making a foil for the applied gemstones and black jet beads.

Detail 120 x 70mm (4¾ x 2¾in)
England, *c.* 1910–20
(Museum of Costume and Textiles, Nottingham)

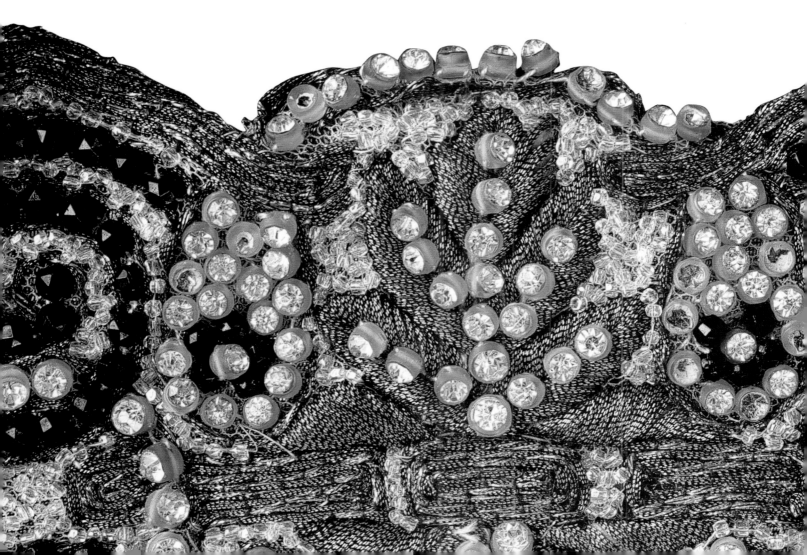

left and right A variety of beads and mounted gemstones are combined with tambour chain embroidery in metal thread on this lined, black satin dress. The beadwork makes the dress very heavy and it would have been uncomfortable for the wearer to sit down. The beads are sewn with a tambour hook from the wrong side of the work. The chain stitch embroidery would be worked from the right side. A superior workshop design.

Detail 110mm sq. (4¼in sq.)
England, *c.* 1925–28
(Embroiderers' Guild Collection)

above Beaded bag with a looped fringe and central tassel. The beads are couched in strung groups onto a fine canvas backing.

150 x 200mm (6 x 8in)
England, *c.* 1920–30
(Gaynor Davies Collection)

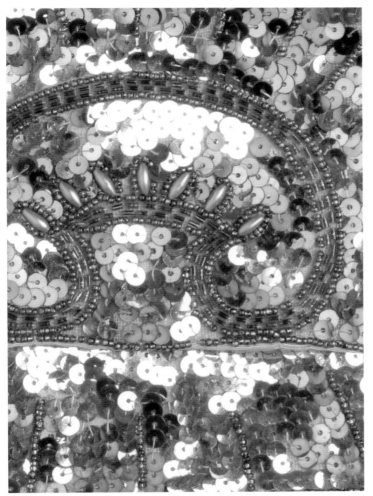

left and above A bead-embroidered bag from
the 1940s combines flat, gold sequins with tiny,
metallic beads and oval pearls to create a sun-burst
design on the front flap, with the rays continued
onto the main bag. Metallic beads outline the
handle and emphasize the side seams.

170 x 110mm (6¾ x 4⅛in)
England, *c.* 1940–1945

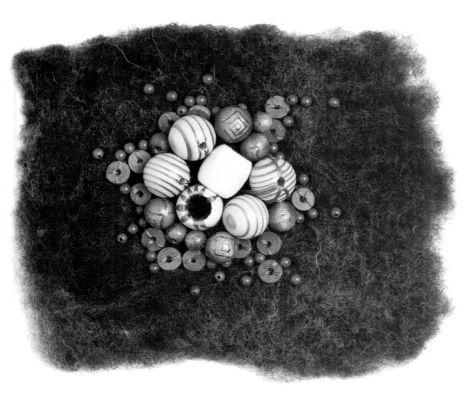

left Experimental sample, with beads applied to a background of handmade felt. The sample uses a variety of wooden beads and washers held with rayon floss thread.

150 x 230mm (6 x 9in)
England, 1990
(Jane Davies)

opposite Beaded cross with a mirror centre, mounted on a box lid. Beads are incorporated in the stitchery of raised chain band, worked over shaped polystyrene.

Detail 80 x 50mm (3¼ x 2in)
England, *c.* 1987
(Jane Lemon)

left Experimental sample using layers of sheer patterned fabrics, with sequins applied behind and on top of the background layer. Long stitches in metallic thread hold the sequins in place.

150 x 230mm (6 x 9in)
England, 1990
(Jane Davies)

47

left Embroidery canvas has been
combined with handmade paper, and
coloured afterwards with silk fabric dyes,
to form a background for hand stitchery
and beadwork. Simple cross-and-star
stitches make use of the canvas grid,
while the French knots and round beads
in two sizes complement the mauves and
orange of the fabric dyes. The rough
paper edges are retained to give a free
texture to the outlines of the piece.
Beads of various types and sizes give
added highlights to the design.

150 x 230mm (6 x 9in)
England, 1990
(*Jane Davies*)

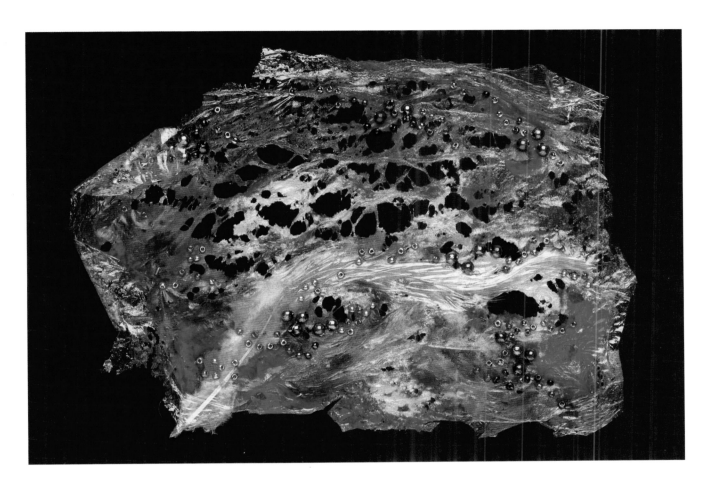

above In this experimental beadwork sample, feathers are sandwiched between two pieces of clingfilm and then placed, over a layer of adhesive web, onto the background fabric. All layers are ironed through parchment paper to prevent the iron from sticking. This adheres and melts part of the clingfilm, both trapping and exposing the feathers. Beads of various types and sizes add highlights to the design.

220 x 160mm (8¾ x 6¼in)
England, 2004
(*Jane Davies*)

49

North America

above Small beaded articles, such as this bead-embroidered needle case, were made for export by the Woodlands Iroquois people of north-east America, featuring the lazy-bead stitch groups sewn over padding onto black velvet. Both round beads and bugle beads in a variety of colours have also been used.

110 x 200mm (4¼ x 8in)
North America, *c.* 1860–70

50

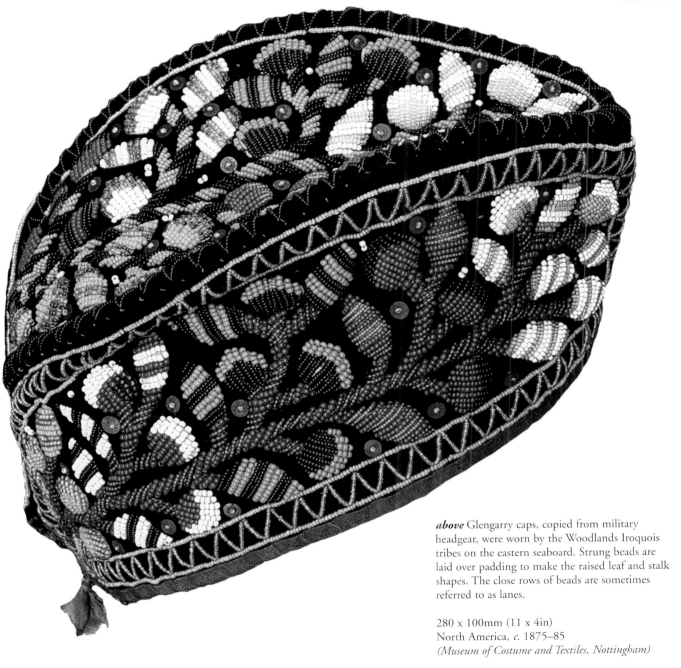

above Glengarry caps, copied from military
headgear, were worn by the Woodlands Iroquois
tribes on the eastern seaboard. Strung beads are
laid over padding to make the raised leaf and stalk
shapes. The close rows of beads are sometimes
referred to as lanes.

280 x 100mm (11 x 4in)
North America, *c.* 1875–85
(Museum of Costume and Textiles, Nottingham)

51

above A pair of moccasins from the Athapaskan
tribes of North America. These delightful shoes
have a pointed toe with a soft sole and fur cuff.
The front tongue and the turned heel cuff are
decorated with couched and laid beads to form
a series of closely stitched diamond patterns.

240mm (9⅖in)
North America, *c.* 1900–1925

52

Central Asia and the East

below This sequined, embroidered tea cosy in red, woollen fabric was made in India, possibly for a Memsahib of the British Raj. Scrolled flowers, embroidered with couched metal threads, are combined with gold and silver sequins to surround the central motif of a golden elephant. The sequins overlap to form clusters of flowers and follow the body lines of the padded elephant.

340 x 270mm (13½ x 10½in)
India, late 19th century

53

above This beaded evening purse from the early
1930s probably comes from the Far East. The
beads are sewn down in strung groups onto a fine
canvas fabric. Chain stitch embroidery in coloured
threads, worked with a tambour hook, enhances
the design motifs.

180 x 100mm (7 x 4in)
The Far East, *c.* 1930–1935

above A dowry purse from Sind, Pakistan,
constructed from a larger rectangle, embroidered
in silks and featuring shisha mirror work, couched
threads and open chain stitch. The four corners
are folded to the middle; the lower corner is held
on both sides with decorative seams, while the
upper corner makes the flap.

190mm sq. (7½in sq.)
Sind, Pakistan, *c.* 1950

left A pistol holster case is decorated with beadwork, fine stitchery and a zip edging. Stem, cross and satin stitches form the zigzag patterns of the ground, while small white beads are sewn singly or in clusters with the addition of larger brass beads. This detail of the pistol holster shows the arrangement of the seed beads that outline the geometric cross stitch patterns.

Detail 100 x 60mm (4 x 2¼in)
Kohistan area, Pakistan, *c.* 1960

right Close-worked buttonhole stitch surrounds the tiny mirrors on this man's Shisha work hat from Pakistan. Lines of couched threads surround the central medallion and define the crown and hat borders.

Diameter 180mm (7in)
Pakistan, *c.* 1970

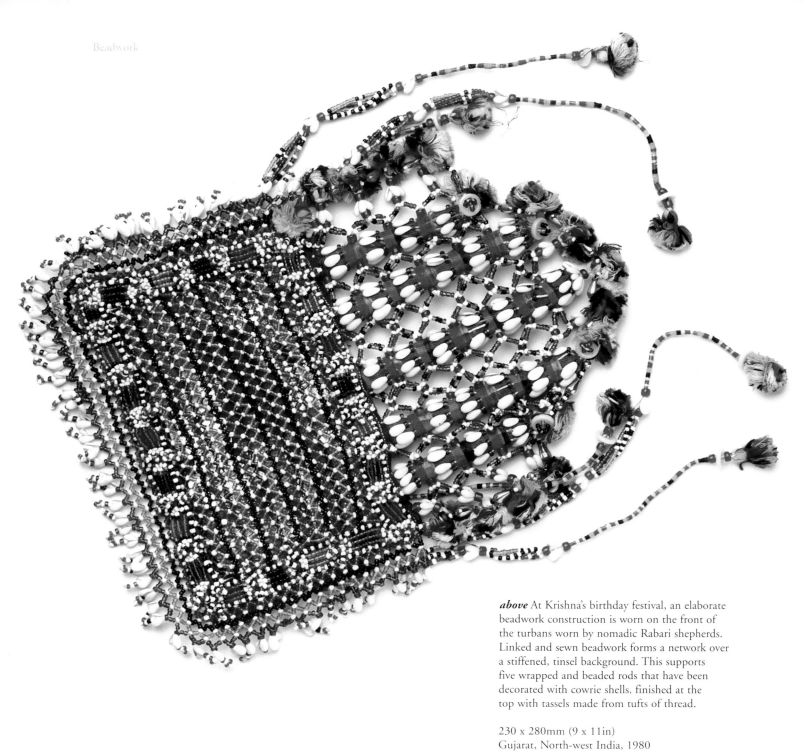

above At Krishna's birthday festival, an elaborate beadwork construction is worn on the front of the turbans worn by nomadic Rabari shepherds. Linked and sewn beadwork forms a network over a stiffened, tinsel background. This supports five wrapped and beaded rods that have been decorated with cowrie shells, finished at the top with tassels made from tufts of thread.

230 x 280mm (9 x 11in)
Gujarat, North-west India, 1980

right The Karen Hill tribe people use little seeds called Job's tears to decorate their clothing and accessories. The seeds are pierced and used as beads, often in combination with hand stitchery. Radiating satin stitches worked in a red cotton thread form alternating squares with the seed beadwork on this small bag. A red silk cord forms a handle and two wool tassels hang down at the sides.

190 x 200mm (7½ x 8in)
North-west Thailand, *c.* 1995

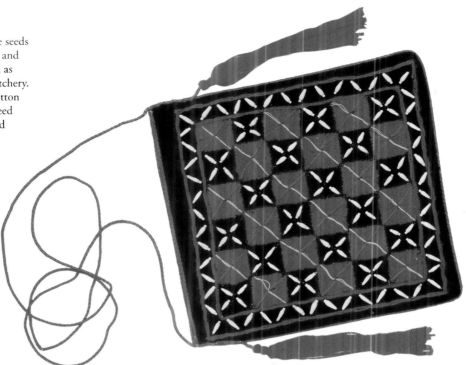

left The original *Kalagas*, or temple wall hangings, came from Burma. Originally depicting scenes from the lives of the Buddha, secular designs were adopted later by the Royal Palaces. Today, adaptations of these pictures, many featuring motifs of sequin-covered animals, are made. This padded elephant, for example, is encircled by couched metallic threads and applied glass beads, together with added groups of sequins.

280mm sq. (11in sq.)
Myanmar (formerly Burma), *c.* 1990

far right This heavily beaded headdress, which resembles an open crown with a long tail, is worn under the outer headdress by the women of the Kalash Valleys. Called a *Kupas*, it is worn every day, even when the women work in the fields, while the outer one is reserved for dance festivals.

right Detail of the *Kupas* headdress. Groups of strung beads are sewn to a woollen background fabric and include cowrie-shells, buttons and little bells. Bead colours and motifs change with fashion.

630 x 110mm (24¾ x 4¼in)
Balanguru Valley, Chitral, Pakistan, 2001

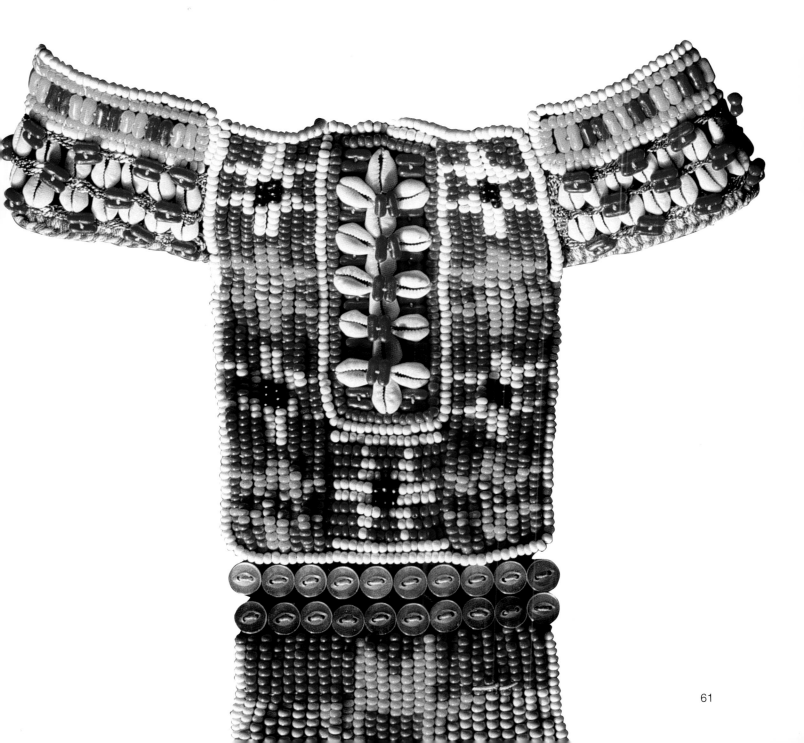

Africa

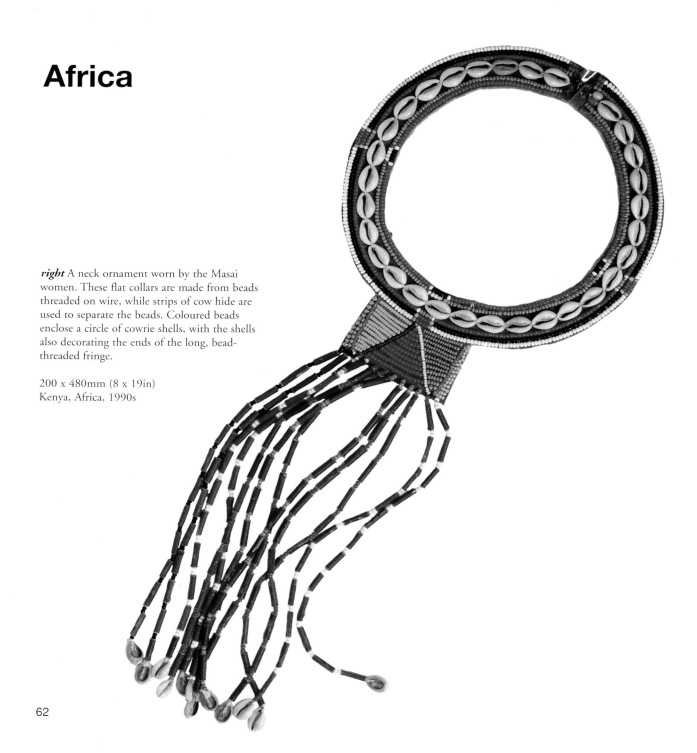

right A neck ornament worn by the Masai women. These flat collars are made from beads threaded on wire, while strips of cow hide are used to separate the beads. Coloured beads enclose a circle of cowrie shells, with the shells also decorating the ends of the long, bead-threaded fringe.

200 x 480mm (8 x 19in)
Kenya, Africa, 1990s

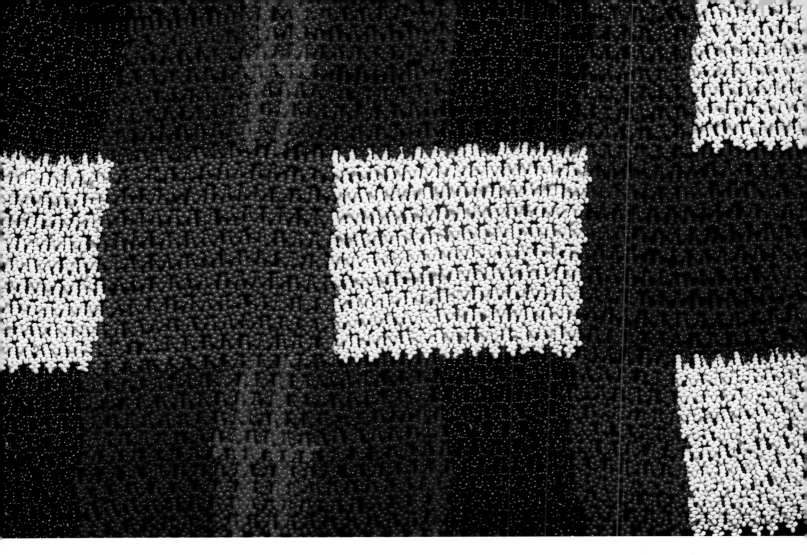

above An unusual, bead-strung technique is
used to make this Zulu Mabintha apron. Starting
from the base line, little bead loops, each with a
three-bead picot in the middle, are sewn to the
background fabric in overlapping rows, rather like
the articulated scales of some reptilian creature.

Detail 290 x 190mm (11½ x 7½in)
South Africa, 1995

Chapter Three
Counted Thread

Europe

right During the 18th century a band was worked by young girls for use as a sample – the forerunner of our modern stitch books. Stitches show cross, Florentine, Holbein double running, needle weaving and pulled thread work. Motifs depict animals, birds, flowers and the alphabet.

Detail 140 x 190mm (5½ x 7½in)
England, 1750

66

left The finest petit point stitches are used to embroider this purse front with a count of 45 stitches to 25mm (1in). The single, linen canvas is mounted on a coarser canvas for greater stability. A typical early 19th-century design of exotic birds, flowers and scenery.

150 x 130mm (6 x 5in)
Possibly French but probably Austrian, *c.* 1810

right Fragment of a bed curtain from the island of Rhodes, Greece. The design shows the traditional *glastra*, or flower pot, worked in heavy silks on linen fabric. Rhodes cross stitch has a raised appearance, possibly the result of stitching over waste canvas, or by working over a rod that is later withdrawn.

150 x 140mm (6 x 5½in)
Greek Islands, 1790–1800

below Even-weave coin net forms the background for floral sprigs and vertical lines on a purse that has been embroidered with wool and silk. Flat stitches and a variation of Hungarian stitch are used for the flowers, while threaded yellow silk is couched down with red wool.

170 x 100mm (6¾ x 4in)
England, *c.* 1825–1830

above Berlin wool work on double-thread canvas, cut from a larger piece, probably a chair cover or seat cushion. Leaf outlines contain smaller motifs worked in different stitches so that cross stitch, mosaic and tent stitch give a change of texture to enhance the floral sprays. Embroidery threads in wool and silk add light and shade to the work.

220mm sq. (8¾ in sq.)
England, *c.* 1850–1860

left The bright, dyed colours date this cross stitch band to after 1856 when William Perkin first patented the new aniline dyes. The combination of roses and fuchsias, first introduced to Kew in 1790, shows an interest in flowers echoed by the hand-painted Berlin wool work patterns. Possibly intended for a mantelpiece or window pelmet.

Detail 430 x 220mm (17 x 8¾in)
England, *c.* 1860

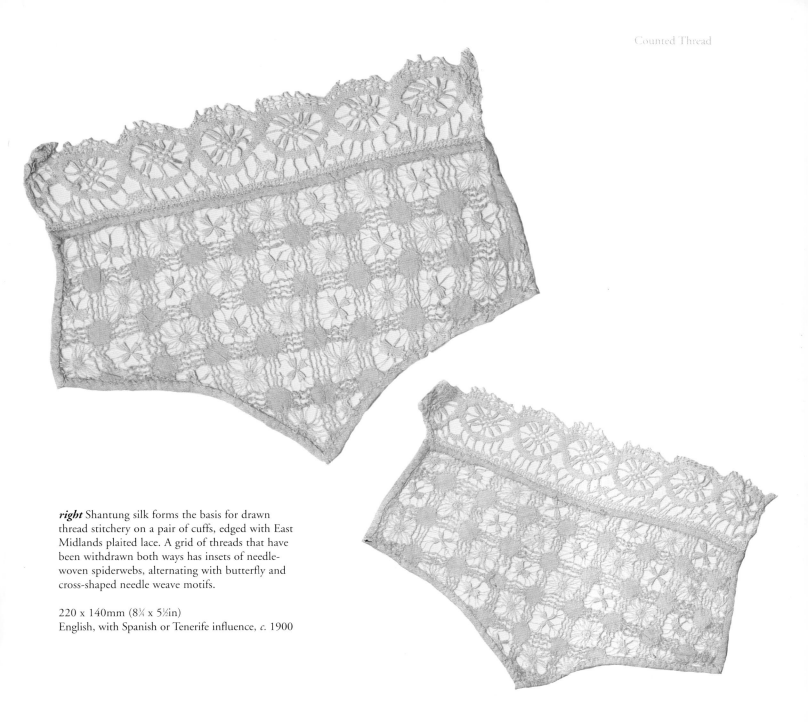

right Shantung silk forms the basis for drawn thread stitchery on a pair of cuffs, edged with East Midlands plaited lace. A grid of threads that have been withdrawn both ways has insets of needle-woven spiderwebs, alternating with butterfly and cross-shaped needle weave motifs.

220 x 140mm (8¾ x 5½in)
English, with Spanish or Tenerife influence, *c.* 1900

71

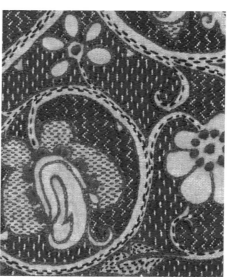

left and below The Jacobean style was chosen by an Edinburgh competitor for this coloured embroidery, possibly designed for a small chair seat or a tea cosy front. The evenly worked stitches include a counted brick stitch, which forms a background for the darned outlines of the arabesque flowers. Chain, padded satin, buttonhole eyelets and seeding stitch make this original design a lively piece – we can only hope that it gained good marks.

350–230 x 260mm (13¾–9 x 10¼in)
Scotland, 1905

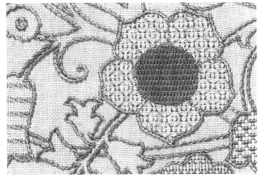

above and right Traditional blackwork stitches
have been worked in Dresden blue on natural,
even weave linen to make a nightdress case.
Stitches include a variety of blackwork fillings,
twisted chain, double buttonhole and hem
stitching for the inner and outer borders. The
corners are mitred, and the hand stitching is
superb, on a piece possibly influenced by the
Arts and Crafts movement.

430 x 300mm (17 x 11⅞in)
England, *c.* 1920

73

above Assisi work in blue, cotton thread decorates
the border of a linen hand towel. There are no
outlines to the motifs, but double-running or
Holbein stitch delineates the bird wings and
eyes, as well as the geometric border patterns.
The opposing bird pairs are flanked on one side
by a tree of life and on the other by a fountain.
Cross stitch fills the background, while hemstitch
and drawn thread are used to secure the hem.

390 x 560mm (15¼ x 22in)
England, *c.* 1920

below A design in Assisi work, which originated
in Italy, is embroidered onto the flap of this linen
handkerchief case. Winged mythical beasts, together
with little birds, flank a central fountain of life.
The outlines of the motifs and the horizontal
borders are worked in double-running stitch,
while cross stitch fills the blue background.

250 x 140mm (9¾ x 5½in)
England, *c*. 1930

75

left Portuguese invaders built fortified castles on
the Atlantic coast of Morocco. Their descendants
settled in Azemmour and introduced a type of
Assisi work embroidery that is unique to this area.
Double-running stitch outlines the voided motifs
of fabulous beasts, while the background is filled
with long-armed cross stitch in dark red or blue.
Fez step stitch is used for both the inner and
outer borders, combining both Italian and
Moroccan techniques.

Detail 140 x 90mm (5½ x 7½in)
Morocco, 1999

above An open weave, cotton fabric has been
used for a woman's cap from Bosnia. The fine
cross stitch embroidery, featuring pomegranate
and leaf motifs, shows designs influenced by
several hundred years of Turkish occupation.
The brim is bordered with needle-worked *oya*
lace triangles.

170 x 480mm (6¾ x 19in)
Bosnia, *c.* 1930

left A woman's cap displays bright, geometric patterns. Gobelin stitch is worked in coloured, silk floss threads on a fine, linen canvas with black outlines in tent stitch. The designs of castellated cross motifs suggest a former Yugoslavian origin.

250 x 370mm (9¾ x 14½in)
Balkan, *c.* 1930

above Inset bands of cross stitch, embroidered
cotton fabric are a feature of Russian folk costume.
These plain bands are embroidered through waste
or surplus canvas that has been laid over the fabric
surface. When the work is finished, the canvas
is dampened and the threads withdrawn to leave
the embroidery intact. The freed stitches have a
slightly raised appearance.

left Navy band with a geometric pattern
Detail 130 x 220mm (5 x 8¾in)

right Red band with roses and leaves
Detail 160 x 220mm (6¼ x 8¾in)

Russia, *c.* 1910–1930

below Cross stitch-embroidered fabric bands of cotton poplin are alternated with deep inserts of torchon bobbin lace on this decorative apron from the Ukraine. The geometric patterns are worked over waste canvas which is removed after the embroidery is finished.

Detail 280 x 380mm (11 x 15in)
Ukraine, *c.* 1910–1930

left An apron in red, cotton fabric is decorated with cross stitch embroidery. This is worked over a waste canvas which is removed when the work is completed. Fabric bands, showing grapevines, daisies with carnation flowers and meandering stems, alternate with insertions of torchon bobbin lace.

400 x 550mm (15¾ x 21⅝in)
Russia, *c.* 1925–1930

above A cottage tea cosy worked on double thread canvas by Daisy Stonehouse. A list of coloured threads, written on an envelope postmarked October 1930, gives an exact date. Cross stitch is used for the cottage walls and the flowers, while upright gobelin adds texture to the thatched roof, finished with a border of buttonhole stitch.

400 x 310mm (15¾ x 12½in)
England, 1930

below Lefkara lace is the name given to the
traditional drawn thread work from Cyprus, while
avalotee, meaning sieve, is an excellent description
of the central motifs where threads are withdrawn
to make the lacework filling stitches. The addition
of satin stitch, eyelets, four-sided stitch and hem
stitching make this mat a very special piece.

440 x 290mm (17¼ x 11½in)
Cyprus, *c.* 1950

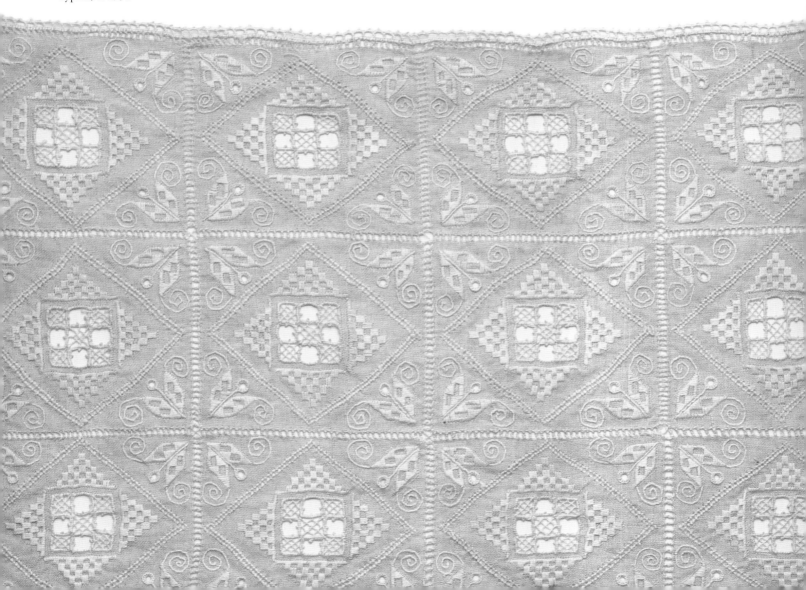

above A pulled work sampler showing a variety
of stitches. Worked on a loose, even weave fabric,
the geometric-patterned open work is achieved
by pulling the threads together, rather than by
withdrawing them.

Detail 150 x 100mm (6 x 4in)
England, 1972
(Angela Thompson)

below One of a pair of cuff pieces from the Balkans. A fine cotton cord in bright colours is used to embroider the geometric border patterns. The unusual stitchery is formed of straight stitch lines, that are later interlinked with a herringbone stitch, that shows only on the surface. Diamond lozenges and the hooked, outer motifs are typical of this region.

150 x 280mm (6 x 11in)
Balkans, *c.* 1950–70

below Geometric embroidery on cotton calico forms a set that was intended for a man's shirt. The uncut pieces comprise the shirt front, collar band and two cuff bands. Turkish step stitch, satin and straight stitches worked in cotton thread and gold and silver cords, form the lozenge and zigzag patterns.

Detail 320 x 210mm (12½ x 8¼in)
Albania, *c.* 1970–1980

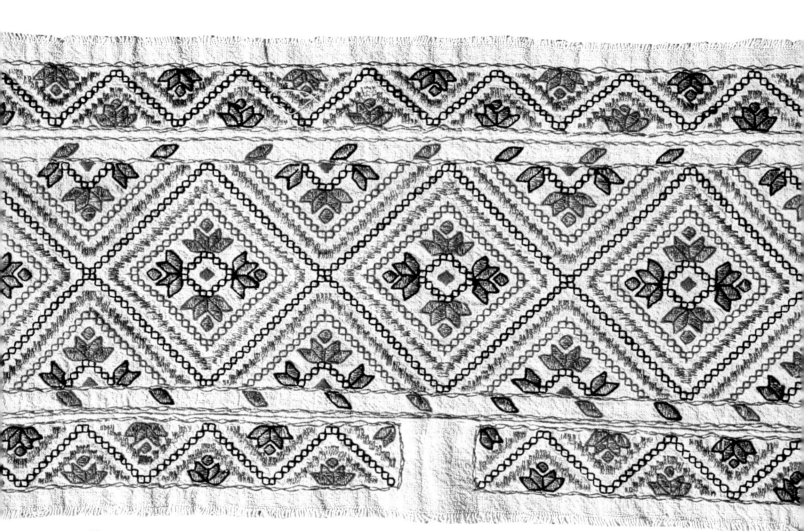

below A counted thread pattern, embroidered in
synthetic silk threads, on a background fabric of
jute is one of the traditions of Eastern Europe.
This tablecloth comes from Lovech and is worked
by a local embroiderer. Satin and cross stitches,
together with double-running stitch, are combined
to form a geometric pattern.

Detail 190 x 150mm (7½ x 6in)
Bulgaria, *c.* 1992

Turkey

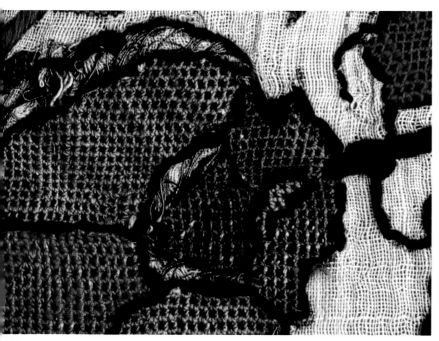

left and below This fragment of embroidery worked onto a soft, cotton fabric contains classic Turkish stitches, now seldom used. Mushabak reversed faggot, Gozeme double running and Sarma satin stitch outline and fill the shapes of the flower petals. The embroidery is the same on both sides.

Detail 65 x 50mm (2½ x 2in)
Turkey, *c.* 1850

right Turkish towels were used as cover cloths for the utilitarian towels when ladies visited the women's baths, a social occasion. Pomegranate flower pot motifs are embroidered with reverse faggot, step stitch and double running outlines in silk floss with metal threads.

Detail 270 x 130mm (10½ x 5in)
Turkey, *c.* 1860

right These little mats were made by Muslim refugees from the Russo-Turkish war of 1877–1880 and sold in Britain by the Turkish Compassionate Fund. Stitches on loose woven cotton include satin stitch, needle weaving, Algerian eye and triangle stitch, worked in cream silks and silver gilt metal cords. The rolled hems are decorated with silk thread tassels.

160mm sq. (6¼in sq.)
Turkey, 1877–1880

Asia and the East

above A bag front, featuring geometric pattern motifs reminiscent of Persian carpet designs, is worked in Smyrna double-cross stitch using embroidery cotton and silks. The mosaic of octagons, squares and triangles is surrounded by borders worked in Ari chain stitch. A 40mm (1½in) twisted fringe is added on three sides.

340 x 320mm (13½ x 12½in)
Uzbekistan, *c.* 1950

right Counted cross stitch is worked onto a closely woven fabric to give a fine-scale example of tribal workmanship. Eight-pointed stars in two sizes dominate the brightly coloured geometric pattern, which contrasts with the deep apricot fabric. The uncut pieces would be used to form a pair of cuffs for a man's shirt.

230 x 240mm (9 x 9½in)
Afghanistan, *c.* 1970

left A Hunza hat embroidered with cross stitch motifs. The motifs on the crown leave plain areas of the cotton background fabric. The side bands are made separately by women in local craft workshops.

Diameter 190mm (7½in)
Northern Pakistan, *c.* 1980

right This cross stitch hat from Karimabad, in the Karakoram mountains, has a little bird motif embroidered on the side band. The Hoopoe bird is both an emblem of protection and also a love charm. Geometric crown patterns resemble the *gul* flowers on Oriental carpets.

Diameter 190mm (7½in)
Northern Pakistan, *c.* 1990–95

below A hat worked in cross stitch by the Hunza women who live in the Karakoram mountain area. Traditional geometric patterns of flowers and leaf shapes are influenced by designs on carpets from Persia and central Asian countries.

Diameter 190mm (7½in)
Chitral, Pakistan, *c.* 1990–2000

above Geometric patterns on this cross stitch
square are part of the design tradition of the Sani
people from the Kunming area in China. The
squares are used as bag panels, apron fronts and as
folded head cloths. Several head cloths are worn at
the same time with only the folded edge showing.
The initial embroidery grid is interpreted freely,
and the worker is not worried if the patterns do
not fit.

300 x 290mm (11¾ x 11½in)
Yunnan Province, South Western China, *c.* 1980

left A Red Miao woman's indigo-dyed jacket from Kongwang village in the Guizhou Province, China. Thick pattern darning in red, silk floss covers the lower back, while cross stitch, tent and upright gobelin stitches are used for the geometric motifs on the upper part. The cross and hooked key-pattern squares form a talisman against danger. Rows of little men, together with goddess figures in cross stitch, form alternating rows as border patterns.

690 x 600mm (27¼ x 23½in)
Guizhou, South-west China, 1995–2000

95

above The scalloped loops of layered, buttonhole stitches on this collar and cuff set may have been added at a later date. The 19th-century embroidery in cotton and silk is worked onto natural linen. The design shows a vase motif with three round flowerheads together with flower and leaf borders. Stitches used include satin, stem, feather, buttonhole, couched fillings, chain and herringbone.

Cuff 210 x 120mm (8¼ x 4⅜in)
Collar 370 x 50mm (14½ x 2in)
Hungary, *c.* 1880

above and right The corner of a tablecloth worked in Anglo-Indian embroidery, the name given to a popular needlework during the late 19th century. The Paisley pattern has a characteristic curved top and decorative fronds. The red background is left unembroidered, and stitches include satin, stem, Romanian couching, herringbone, Cretan, feather and buttonhole.

1040mm sq. (41in sq.)
England, *c.* 1875–1885

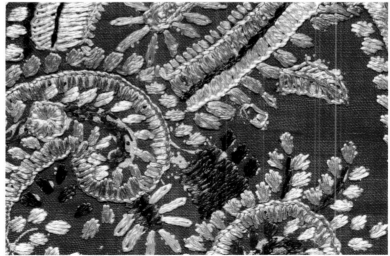

above and right A square cloth worked in
Anglo-Indian embroidery. The red, ground fabric
is entirely covered with stitchery in a heavy, silk
thread with some cotton. Stitches are limited
to satin, stem and chain and a black silk fringe
is sewn around the border. Stitchery worked
on a printed fabric was probably influenced by
Leek embroidery, worked on damask patterned
silk fabric.

Detail 230 x 160mm (9 x 6¼in)
England, *c.* 1875–1885

104

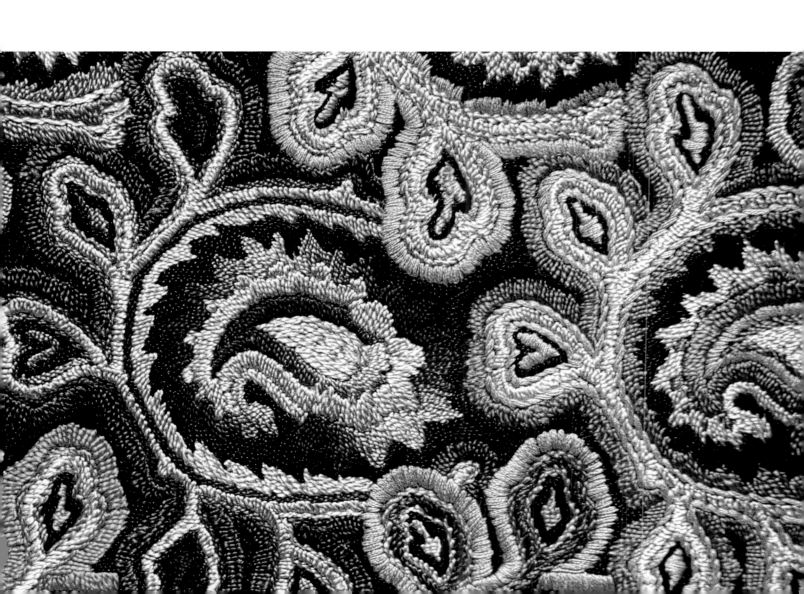

left and below Corner detail of a part-worked
Anglo-Indian cloth, where heavy stitchery covers
most of the printed surface. Stitches include
buttonhole, chain, stem and rosette chain. The
stitches are embroidered through two fabric layers.

Detail 250 x 190mm (9¾ x 7½in)
England, *c.* 1885–1895

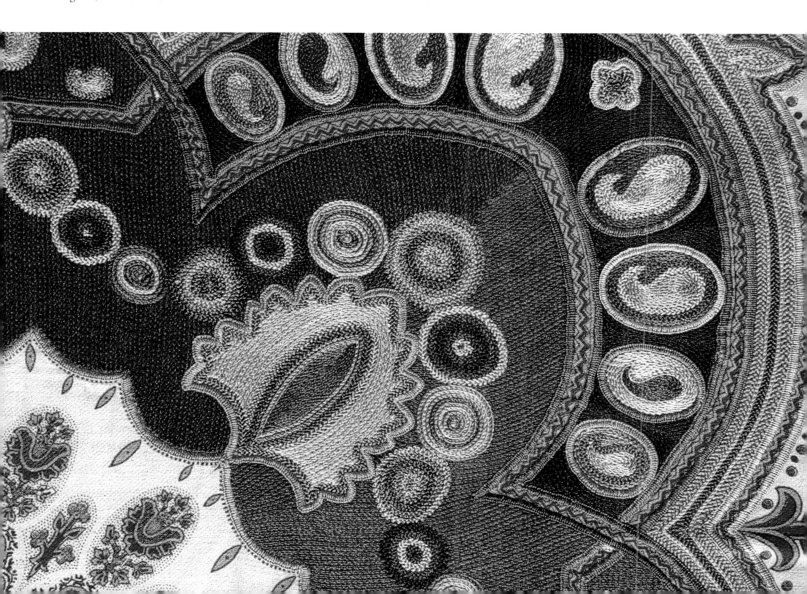

above An Art Nouveau tea cosy is made in the fashionable, angular shape. The cream silk fabric is embroidered with floss silk threads to show a mirrored design of twining stems with rose and leaf sprays. Stitches include satin, Romanian couching and speckling. Faint blue transfer lines are still visible, which show that this was a commercial pattern.

360–270 x 250mm (14¼–10½ x 9¾in)
England, 1895–1900

below Northern Hungary is famous for the Matyo flower embroidery, worked by an agricultural community who wished to rise above their poverty. Bright, silk floss threads are embroidered onto the black festival aprons worn by the men. The use of this decorative square is unknown, but it is typical of the satin-stitched embroidery which covers the entire ground.

410mm sq. (16¼in sq.)
Hungary, *c.* 1920

left Double aprons, in the form of separate front and back skirts, are a feature of eastern European folk costume. Both aprons are the same size, and the front apron overlaps the back one. Naturalistic designs are hand-embroidered in white cotton cord onto black satin fabric, together with scrolling patterns in yellow tamboured chain stitch.

650 x 1200mm (25½ x 47¼in)
Slovakia, 1920–1925

right The front of a small bag, made from natural linen, is embroidered with floral motifs in circular coiling stems, with tendrils and curved leaves that are reminiscent of Elizabethan stitchery. This revival dates from the 1920s, when styles from the past became popular. Stitches include satin, stem, buttonhole, feather, fern, couching and French knots.

Detail 160 x 110mm (6¼ x 4¼in)
England, *c.* 1920–1930
(Diana Banks Collection)

above Greek-style, geometric motifs are embroidered onto an envelope bag made of linen crash fabric, using silk and woollen threads. Satin stitch, stem, pattern darning and threaded running stitch show the influence of folk embroidery during the early 1930s.

180 x 150mm (7 x 6in)
England, 1930

above A selection of hand embroidery stitches
– encroaching satin, buttonhole and fly stitch –
are faithfully copied and interpreted as machine
embroidery by the Swiss, who are famous for their
expertise with trade machines. The four segments
of this felt cap are embroidered with flowers in
red, white and blue, with leaves and fronds in
green and yellow.

Diameter 230mm (9in)
Switzerland, 1935

113

left The cover for the back of a chair is embroidered with a spray of flowers, probably from a transfer pattern. The oval flowerheads and colouring are typical of the 1930s. Stitches include cross, stem and padded satin. Threads have been withdrawn on the lower border and filled with decorative, needle weave stitches.

350 x 760mm (14 x 13⅜in)
England, 1935–1940

right These little upright, flowers on stalks are typical of 1960s design. A tray cloth in grey synthetic fabric is embroidered in orange, brown and white with stranded silks. The varied stitches include chain, back stitch, stem, running, fly stitch and bullion knots. The double hem is hand-stitched.

410 x 600mm (16¼ x 23½in)
England, *c.* 1960

left A white, organdie tablecloth is embroidered in silk threads to depict a selection of wild animals, including a giraffe and an impala deer. Stem stitch and encroaching satin stitch are used for the animal bodies, while the background details are in shadow work, using double backstitch, which reverses to herringbone stitch.

1040mm sq. (41in sq.)
England, *c.* 1950

opposite Architecture was the inspiration for this window design where a sandwich of fabric layers, including both shiny and dull materials, are topped with chiffon, then machine-stitched through on the design lines. Different layers are cut away to reveal the fabric underneath, after which hand stitchery and beads are added. The fabric edging has been teased out to give a distressed look.

180mm sq. (7in sq.)
England, 1996
(Jane Davies)

left Both Indian embroidery and English Log Cabin patchwork were the design-source for an experimental piece where dyed, plain and patterned fabrics are first laid in strips, seamed together and cut into triangles. These are then re-applied onto a dyed cotton background and embroidered with straight, chain, feather and herringbone stitches together with French knots, beads and sequins.

Detail 200 x 330mm (8 x 13in)
England, 1999–2000
(Jane Davies)

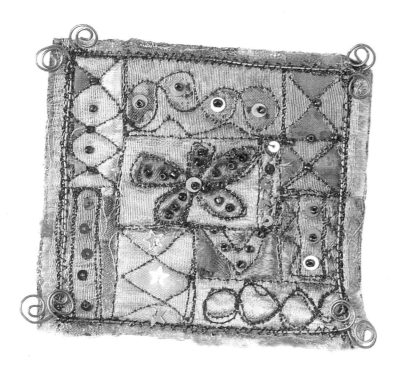

left Double-sided bonding web is ironed onto the felt background, the paper peeled off and rectangles of shiny and fancy fabrics applied. A layer of sheer fabric is ironed on top to hold, then the snippets of fabric are machined round. Machine embroidery, hand stitchery, beads and sequins are added next. Finally, copper wire is zigzagged carefully to the edge by machine.

80mm sq. (3¼in sq.)
England, 2001
(Jane Davies)

right Snippets of sheer voile fabric are applied to a felt background by using a fine-tipped craft soldering-iron to draw along the edges and melt the two layers together. A top layer of voile is fixed by drawing grid-lines with the iron, fusing all the layers. Holes are made through the layers by using the tip of the iron and hand stitches, machine embroidery and beads are added to the surface.

90mm sq. (3½in sq.)
England, 2002
(Jane Davies)

right A fun sampler making use of assorted
fabrics and threads found in the scrap-drawer.
Space-dyed cotton fabric, towelling, tape and
threads are couched onto the background. Silk
rods are ironed flat, cut into strips and applied
with decorative stitches, while pre-dyed feathers
add the finishing touch.

Detail 140 x 90mm (5½ x 3½in)
England, 2004
(*Jane Davies*)

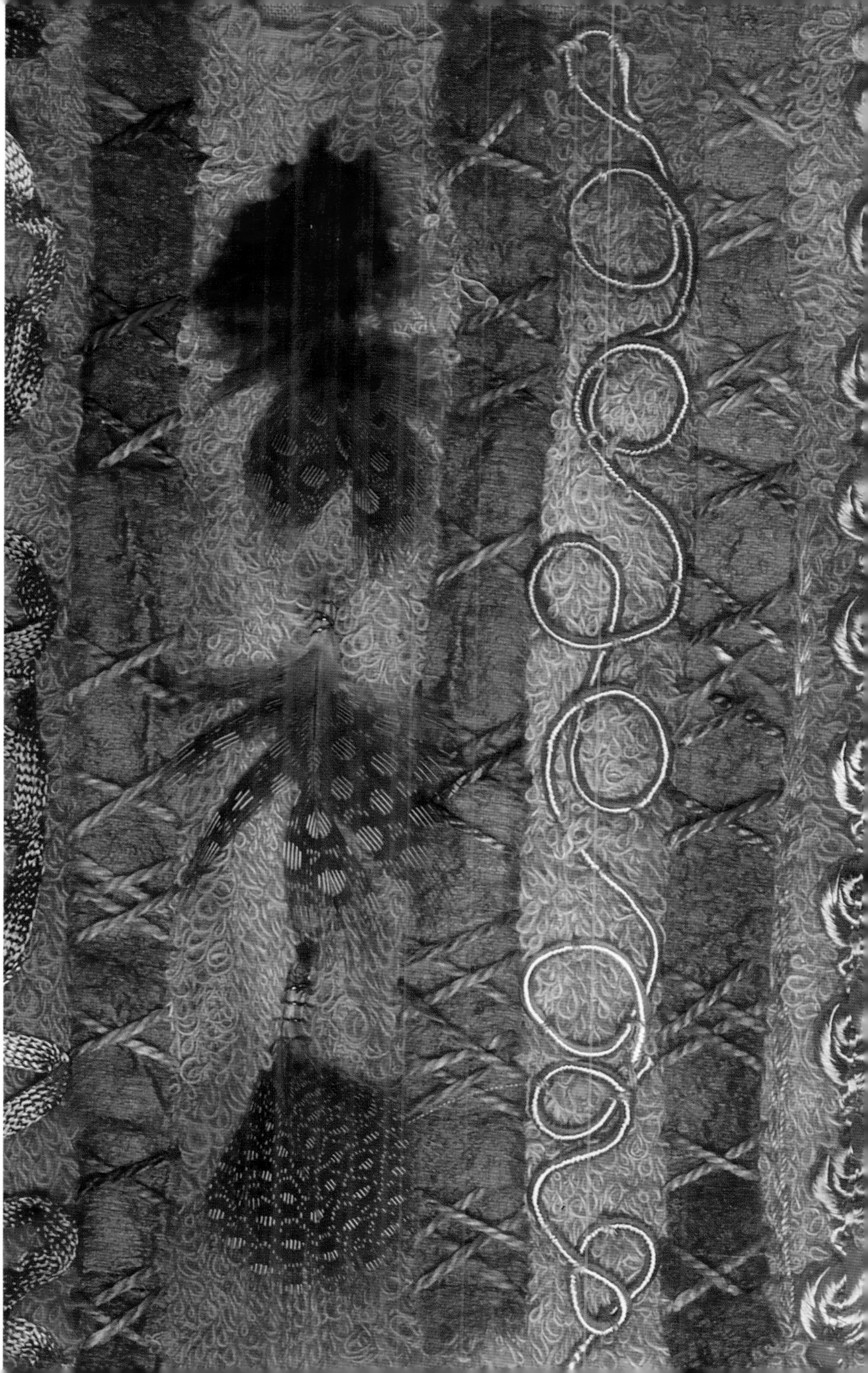

left and right The men of the Dunajec Gorge in southern Poland still wear their traditional embroidered jackets when punting barges down the river. At one time they carried produce and livestock, now the ride is a tourist treat. The embroidery, worked in soft cotton cord and stranded threads, enlivens the front of the sleeveless jacket with floral bands, motifs and pocket decoration.

450 x 560mm (17¾ x 22in)
Southern Poland, 2000

above and right The back of the barge man's jacket shows the floral motifs which differ from jacket to jacket, but are always placed in the same position. In the past, the trousers, jackets and coats were made of heavy wool felt, today the embroidery is worked onto a dark-coloured napped woollen cloth. Stitches are chain, feather, lazy daisy, satin, stem and lines of zig-zag.

450 x 670mm (17¾ x 26⅛in)
Southern Poland, 2000

above and left A little boy's sleeveless jacket is just like the one his father wears. Sequins are added to the flower embroidery to give it extra sparkle and decorative borders outline the edges of the lined garment, which is made without front fastenings.

370 x 430mm (14½ x 17in)
Dunajec Gorge, Southern Poland, 2000

123

Central America

left and right The Guatemalan women living near the volcanic Lake Atitlán embroider their woven *huipil* blouses with floral designs influenced by traditional Spanish patterns. The embroidery is worked in shaded cotton threads giving the roses, carnations and pansies a naturalistic feel. Stitches include satin, stem and long-and-short.

Detail 220 x 140mm (8½ x 5½in)
Guatemala, 1994

above A floral design embroidered onto the front of child's dress in the Oaxaca area of Mexico is neatly worked. Stranded embroidery cotton is used to work the padded satin stitch, stem and backstitch. The use of black adds cohesion to the mixed colours of the flowers.

Detail 308 x 198mm (12¼ x 7⅜in)
Mexico, 2001

Morocco

below Embroidery from Tétouan in northern Morocco is heavily influenced by Turkish design. This distinctive, rare silk *tensifa* fragment has stylized flower and vase motifs embroidered in double darning and satin stitch onto a yellow silk ground. The embroidery is completely reversible.

Detail 100 x 75mm (4 x 3in)
Morocco, *c.* 1890

left and below Fragment of a curtain from Rabat,
used on ceremonial occasions, possibly for a
marriage. Floss silks in aniline dye colours are
used to work a pattern of leaf-fronds onto a light,
cotton muslin which has first been embroidered
with meandering lines of tamboured chain. Satin
stitch and fishbone stitch are worked in closely
packed clumps.

Detail 100 x 110mm (4 x 4¼in)
Morocco, *c.* 1880–1890

Iran and Central Asia

left The name *Suzani* comes from the Persian for needle, which in time referred to the embroidered dowry cloths made by the bride and her family. They took the form of bedcovers, curtains and hangings and a new set was made for each generation. This flaming sun motif, which is reminiscent of fractal patterns, is embroidered in Bukhara couching.

660 x 500mm (26 x 19⅝in)
Uzbekistan, late 19th century
(*Decorative Arts Museum, Tashkent*)

above The floral design on this *Suzani* is indicative of the love of flowers and the importance of gardens in an arid landscape. A variety of stitches may be used. Basma is a laid stitch couched at intervals by the same thread, also known as Bokhara couching. In a second version, a single couching stitch lays parallel to the first one, while Ilmok is another name for our open-chain or ladder stitch.

660 x 500mm (26 x 19⅝in)
Uzbekistan, late 19th century
(*Decorative Arts Museum, Tashkent*)

left Kerman embroidery comes from an
area south west of the city of Isfahan and is
traditionally sewn by women for domestic use as
cloths, bed covers and curtains. Stem stitches are
embroidered onto a fine, woollen cloth to outline
favourite floral motifs, reminiscent of designs
on Persian carpets. Kerman stitch, worked as an
up-and-down satin stitch, is used for the fillings.

Detail 380 x 395mm (15 x 15½in)
Iran, 1860–70

right An octagonal mat worked in a modern
version of Azerbaijan embroidery, using rayon
floss threads. The original, fine scale work was
from Rasht in northern Iran, a port by the
Caspian sea. Blocks of satin stitch fill the motifs
and are outlined with straight stitches or bundles
of couched threads.

360mm (14¼in)
Iran, 2004

left and above A patchwork assembly of old embroidery pieces from Iran, cut from garments and furnishing fabrics. The modern method of couching with white thread bundles is similar to the Azerbaijan embroidery. Detail shows mirror work, couched metallic cords and an unusual embroidery technique combining little white beads with rows of double chain and rosette chain to form hooked outlines.

360mm sq. (14¼in sq.)
Iran, assembled in 2004

India

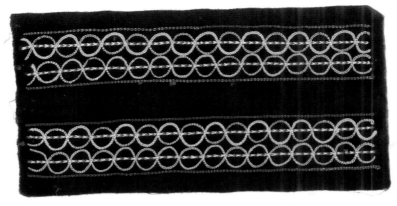

above Slipper uppers and heel pieces ready for assembly are a skilful example of Mochi chain stitchery embroidered by the Kutch untouchable tribes who worked with leather. An Ari hook is used for the fine chain-stitching in silk threads on black velvet.

320 x 170mm (12½ x 6¾in)
Gujarat, North-west India, *c.* 1910

above Detail of a dress front panel from Rajasthan. Geometric outlines include areas of cross stitch, buttonhole, open chain and Romanian couching. The interlacing stitch is indicative of embroidery from this area, possibly brought by German Missionaries to the western coast of India during the 19th century.

Detail 100 x 650mm (4 x 25½in)
Rajasthan, India, *c.* 1980–1990

right Circular cushion cover, designed by Visakha Wijeyeratne, Sri Lanka. The bird motif is cut from a single fabric piece, applied to the background and outlined with open chain stitches. Chain, wheat ear and straight stitches enhance this lively bird, cleverly adapted to fill the circle shape.

Diameter 400mm (15⅞in)
Sri Lanka, *c.* 1985–1990

China

above A waist purse is suspended from a belt by the loop. The black silk satin weave fabric is embroidered in twisted silks, using couched cords, couched metal threads and Pekin knots to make a central pattern of flowers and water weed, flanked by bats which are regarded as symbols of happiness.

100 x 80mm (4 x 3¼in)
China, 1880–1890

left Someone must have regarded this motif showing a pavilion, water bridge and pine tree as very special, for the exquisitely stitched Pekin knot embroidery has been cut out and applied to a hand-made paper backing. The original piece is worked on a silk repp weave fabric, using embroidery silks and gold-wrapped metal threads.

100 x 115mm (4 x 4½in)
China, 1870–1880

below A sleeve band, embroidered with butterflies and flowers, has been cut in half and applied to a silk handkerchief sachet, probably about 1910. Lotus flowers, peonies and ten butterflies are beautifully worked in long-and-short stitch, split chain, straight stitch and couching. Cord bundles are couched to the band edges and around the sachet.

250mm sq. (9¾in sq.)
China, 1880–1890

left Japanese gold thread is couched onto blue-green silk, forming a close-packed design of peonies, begonia leaf sprays and four butterflies.

centre Blue, white and green embroidery silks are used for satin and surface-satin stitches, as well as the back-stitch outlines. Two butterflies nestle within peony flowers and lotus buds, embroidered onto damask-patterned silk in a pale yellow-green.

right A superbly embroidered band of apricot silk, with a design of peonies, begonias and butterflies. Floss silk is used for the long-and-short, satin, stem, back, tied-satin, star and split stitches.

50–80 x 1220mm (2–3¼ x 48in)
China, 1880–1890

below This pictorial embroidery on red silk is likely to have been cut from a skirt panel. A mythical lion-dragon, a symbol of valour, is placed within a landscape that includes stylized waves (the home of dragons), a rock (meaning permanence), a pine tree (longevity), a flaming pearl (representing the power of the dragon), and a bat (a symbol of happiness).

350 x 340mm (13¾ x 13½in)
China, 1890

141

above Detail of a skirt panel showing a
mythical lion-dragon with ferocious teeth
and wild eyes. The tail and mane are worked
in satin stitch, while long-and-short stitch,
outlined with metal threads, is used to fill
the body. Fan stitch is used in a descriptive
manner for the needles of the pine trees.

China, 1890

142

above A detail from the same skirt panel, showing
the use of shading in floss silk embroidery. The
exquisite shading is achieved with satin and
long-and-short stitches. On the left, waves curve
and spray, while on the right, the Karst limestone
rock has voided areas. A magnolia flower sits in
the middle.

China, 1890

143

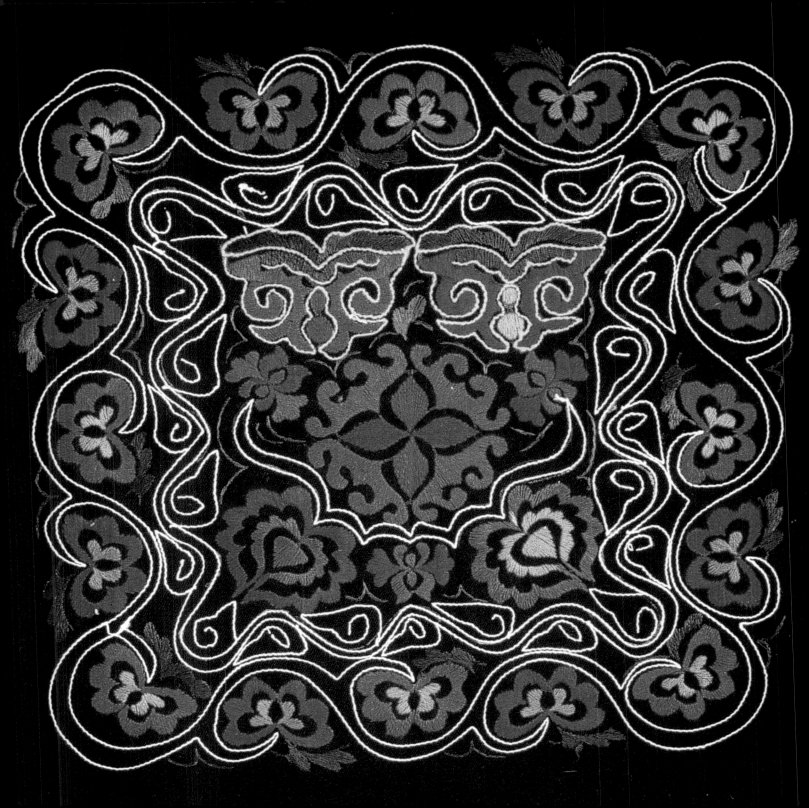

left A decorative square from Yunnan Province is embroidered in satin stitch. The stem stitched white outlines contrast with the black fabric ground giving a three-dimensional effect to the typical Chinese-style floral motifs. The squares are sold as cushion covers, but the original use was for head squares, or for placing on bags, aprons and baby carriers.

410mm sq. (16¼in sq.)
South-west China, c. 1985–1990

below A five-clawed Dragon twists across the lacquer-red silk of an embroidered bag front. A flaming pearl, chrysanthemums and a rock fill the background. Silks are used for surface satin and star stitches, while gold-wrapped, metal threads outline the motifs and hold the laid silk threads of the Dragon's body.

150 x 140mm (6 x 5½in)
China, 1900–1920

left and right Floss silk embroidery is used to decorate the central panel of an apron. Satin stitch and shaded long-and-short stitch are used together with couched braids to portray a series of animals, exotic birds and butterflies. Included are a buffalo at the lower end and a pair of mythical sea dragons near the top.

Detail 90 x 200mm (3½ x 8in)
Guizhou Province, China, *c.* 1980–1990

above Sleeve detail on a festive jacket which is worn with a decorated tab skirt by the women of Taigiang County. Narrow braids, woven on a small loom, are couched in spirals to form the dragon-motif, together with flowers and leaves. Sequins are added and couched metal threads outline the main design areas.

Detail 130 x 150mm (5 x 6in)
Guizhou Province, South-west China, *c.* 1980–1990

right The front of a bag from Shidong shows a typical design of opposing dragons at the top and a pair of buffalo at the lower edge. Embroidery in floss silks using satin stitch, stem stitch and some couching is typical of this area. The lower part of the bag shows the buffalo pair with little birds perched on their backs or playing under the dancing hooves.

Detail 130 x 124mm (5 x 4⅞in)
Eastern Guizhou, China, *c.* 1980–1990

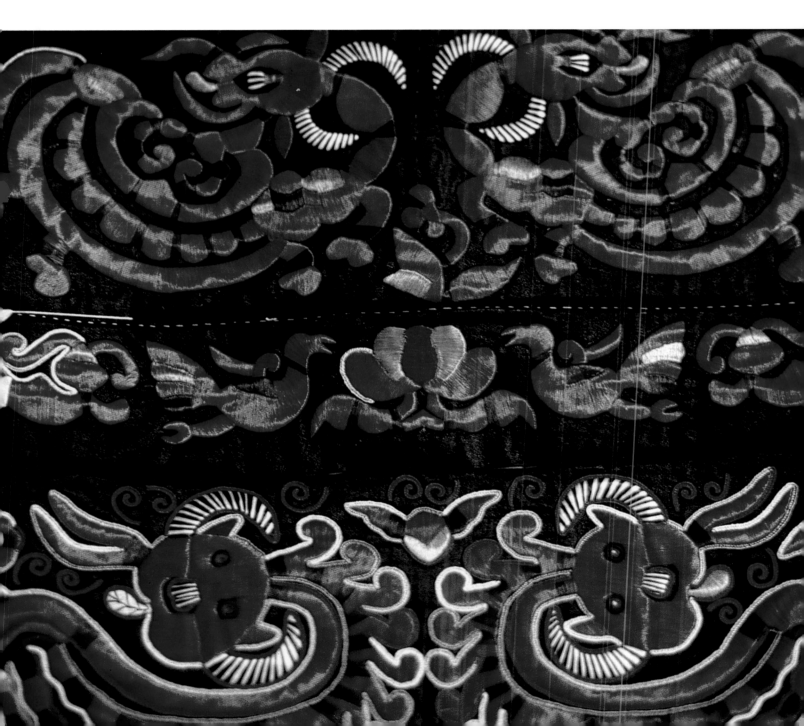

Chapter Five
Goldwork

Europe

left A fragment from a Chasuble, using couched, metal thread on ivory, silk satin. A cartouche holds a foliate leaf and flower design with curved stems and fronds. Embroidered in floss silks using chain, knotted chain and couched, twisted and padded gold threads. Labelled 'Fine English Ecclesiastical Needlework' this piece is representative of the Church embroidery revival.

Detail 165 x 115mm (6½ x 4⅛in)
England, *c.* 1840–50

left Joined fragments of Leek embroidery give an indication of the high standard of work produced under the tuition of Elizabeth Wardle. The wife of the silk merchant Thomas Wardle, she introduced the idea of working ecclesiastical embroidery onto the damask-patterned fabrics produced in her husband's silk-weaving workshops.

Detail 115 x 100mm (4½ x 4in)
Leek, England, *c.* 1880

above An ecclesiastical design on a stole end is
worked in typical Leek embroidery style. The
damask-patterned, silk fabric makes a rich foil for
the immaculately laid gold threads. The long-and-
short satin stitchery, worked in naturally dyed
raw-silks, is a testament to the embroiderer's art.

Detail 80 x 40mm (3¼ x 1½in)
Leek, England, *c.* 1880

153

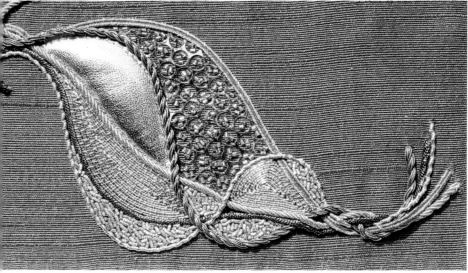

above Detail from a bag front, probably in Leek embroidery. Gold threads outline the wild silk floss, embroidered onto a background of raw silk. Naturally dyed floss silks are typical of this work. William Morris studied fabric dyes in Thomas Wardle's workshop, and many of the Leek embroidery designs show his influence.

Detail 120 x 80mm (4¾ x 3¼in)
Leek, England, *c.* 1885

left Five different gold cords are twisted and splayed out to form the shell shape, filled with couched metal cords, sequin waste, padded kid and small pieces of rough purl, sewn down as beads.

160 x 110mm (6¼ x 4¼in)
England, 1975
(Angela Thompson)

154

above A sheaf of corn is used as the central panel of an altar front for the Church of St John the Baptist, Wellington, Somerset, UK. Gold cords outline the ribbed golden fabric, while gold and bronze beads represent the ripe corn.

760mm sq. (30in sq.)
England, *c.* 1985
(Jane Lemon with Catherine Talbot)

left Detail of a Royal Yacht *Britannia* badge. Smooth purl golden threads are couched over padding to form the outer wreath. Pearl-purl outlines the raised circumference of the globe. Silk threads colour the Union flag and represent the red velvet cap inside the padded crown.

40 x 70mm (1½ x 2¾in)
England, 1990s

right A badge from a cap, which was once worn by an officer serving on the recently decommissioned Royal Yacht *Britannia*. Smooth purl gold thread is used for the lettering and coloured silks cover the padded crown. Known as wire work, heavy metal thread embroidery was worked mainly by men.

80 x 35mm (3¼ x 1⅜in)
England, 1990s

below Sampler showing different gold work embroidery methods. Sequin waste is threaded with strips of gold kid, or combined with small beads and embroidered French knots. Fine gold thread holds golden stars or outlines triangles of padded kid. Golden discs are surrounded with cup sequins, check purl and couched pearl-purl.

Detail 210 x 150mm (8¼ x 6in)
England, 1990
(Jane Davies)

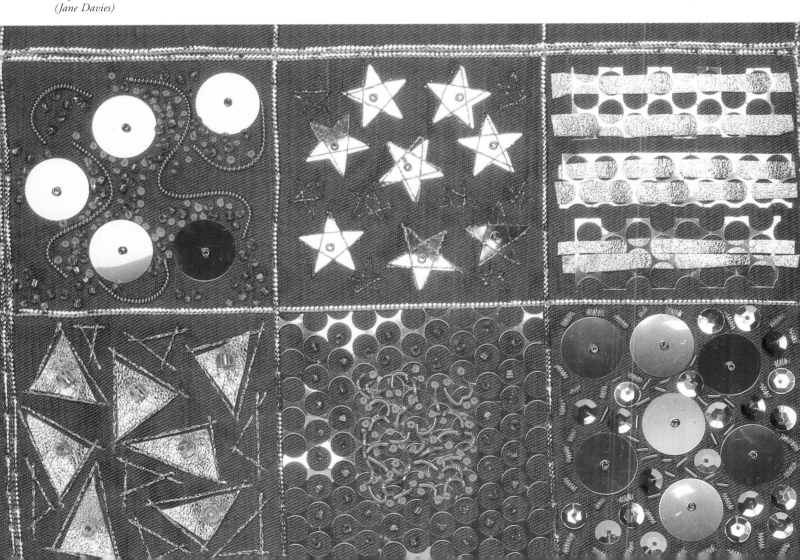

Turkey

above Metal threads are embroidered onto fine silk, cut from the end of a scarf. Golden cords and gold plate are couched to form a design of leaves, flowers and swags. Crystal gemstones form the flower stamens. The flat, narrow gold plate is folded backwards and forwards and the folds are held down with couching stitches.

Detail 200 x 100mm (8 x 4in)
Turkey, *c.* 1850

above Undulating stems with pomegranates and
flower buds form the decoration on this loosely
woven cotton scarf or veil. Stitches worked in metal
threads and embroidery silks combine counted
fillings with satin stitch and double running.

Detail 280 x 170mm (11 x 6¾in)
Turkish Albania, *c.* 1870

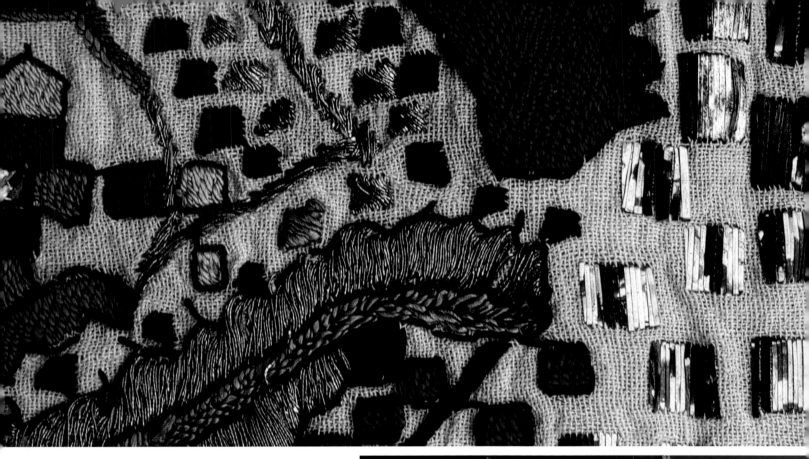

above and right A loosely woven Turkish towel is embellished with blocks of gold and silver plate that surround the two embroidered flower and feather motifs. A fringe of twisted threads, together with a border of satin stitch triangles, decorate both ends of the towel. Horizontal stripes of natural silk are set into the cotton fabric at intervals, making this a special item, possibly for a wedding celebration. A detail of the Turkish towel shows the gold plate taken through the ground fabric, and the fine, gold cord used for the feather fronds. Stitches used are satin, Gozeme double run and Seyrek Sira filling stitch.

Detail 50 x 90mm (2 x 3½in)
Turkey, *c.* 1890

160

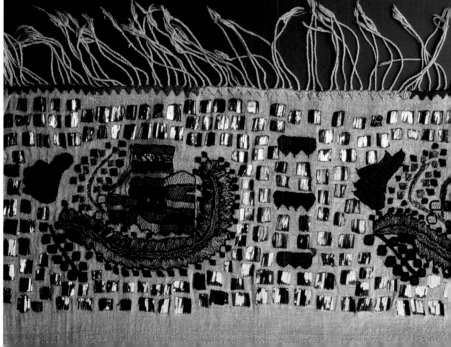

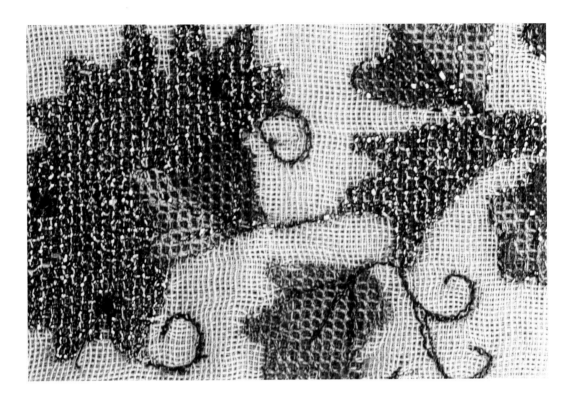

above A loosely woven, cotton fabric provides
the background for fine scale counted thread
embroidery on a modern Turkish veil. A thin, gold
cord, together with shaded machine embroidery
cotton, is used to work the traditional reverse
faggot, double run and Susma step stitch on a
typical, floral motif.

Detail 110 x 90mm (4¼ x 3½in)
Turkey, 1985

India and Pakistan

left Pieces of the shiny, green outer carapace that covered the wings of a beetle are used instead of gemstones to add colour to metal thread embroidery worked onto stiffened cotton gauze. Tablecloths and mats formed the main choice for this type of decoration.

right and below A detail of the round mat shows the pierced beetle wings held by cotton thread. Satin stitches in coloured floss silks fill the flower petals. A double line of couched gold thread is split at intervals to form petal outlines and the leaf bud loops.

Diameter 160mm (6¼in)
Madras, India, *c.* 1875

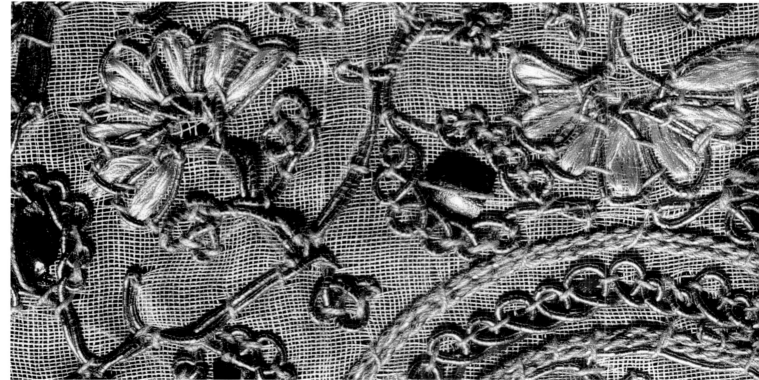

above Loops of couched gold thread form the background lines around the flower motifs and beetle wing leaves on this square mat. Surface satin stitch fills the flower petals in green, pink and turquoise silk floss. Double gold threads define the flower stalks and a twisted, gold, cord fringe is sewn round the four edges.

240mm sq. (9½in sq.)
Madras, India, *c.* 1875

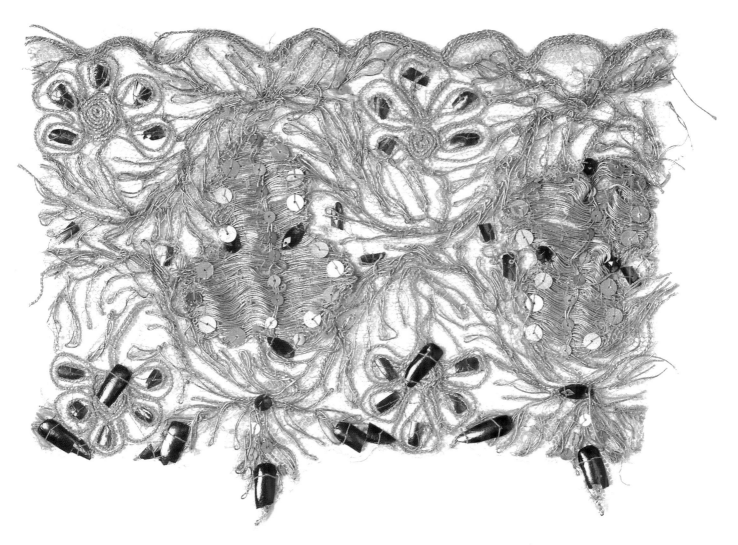

above The iridescent beetle wings were often incorporated into evening dress embroidery. A repeat design of leaf shapes, alternating with flowers, may have formed part of the cotton tulle skirt of a special ball gown. Dark green beetle wings are combined with golden sequins and red beads to form part of the decoration.

210 x 140mm (8¼ x 5½in)
Madras, India, *c.* 1875

165

left and right A fine, white cotton fabric is used as a background for this superbly embroidered tablecloth. A floral pattern of gold thread work is repeated on all four corners, while a scrolling border of golden buds is outlined by drawn thread bands stitched with a fine gold thread. A detail shows the central flower of the corner pattern. Five-strand bundles of real gold threads are couched to form the design outlines, while the flower centres are worked in a pulled-thread stitch called *Jali*. The name refers to the lattice that was used to cover the windows of the women's Purdah quarters.

Detail 40 x 33mm (1½ x 1¼in)
Madras, India, *c.* 1875

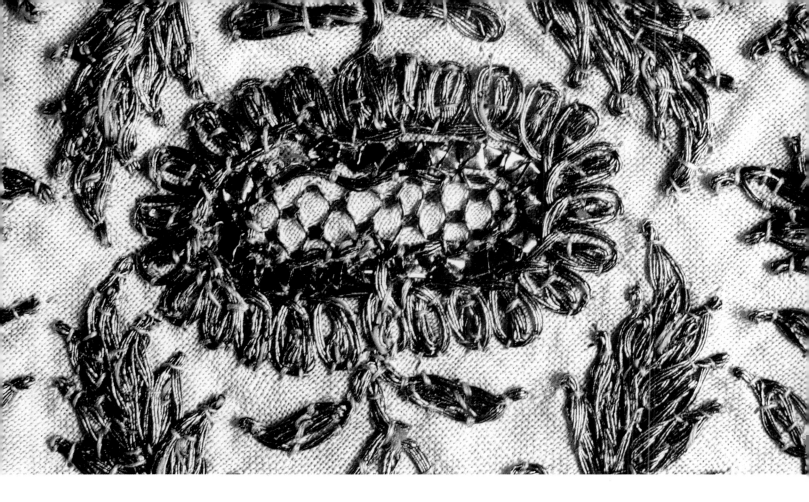

above A heavily padded tea cosy is covered with
an intricate type of metal thread embroidery,
possibly brought by the Portuguese to Goa. Flower
and leaf motifs follow undulating stems to form
the central cartouche. Raised work and couching
are combined with floss silk stitchery. Court
embroiderers, made redundant by the British
Raj, produced their art on domestic articles.

360 x 260mm (14¼ x 10¼in)
Goa, India, *c.* 1890

right An embroidered front for a tea cosy that was
never completed. Areas of basket stitch are worked
in metal threads over a padding to form three
pointed leaf shapes. In between are silk floss
embroidered flowers, using surface satin stitch.
Couched trails of gold thread fill the background
surface. All is finished with a twisted fringe of
golden cord.

340 x 220mm (13½ x 8¾in)
Goa, India, *c.* 1890

168

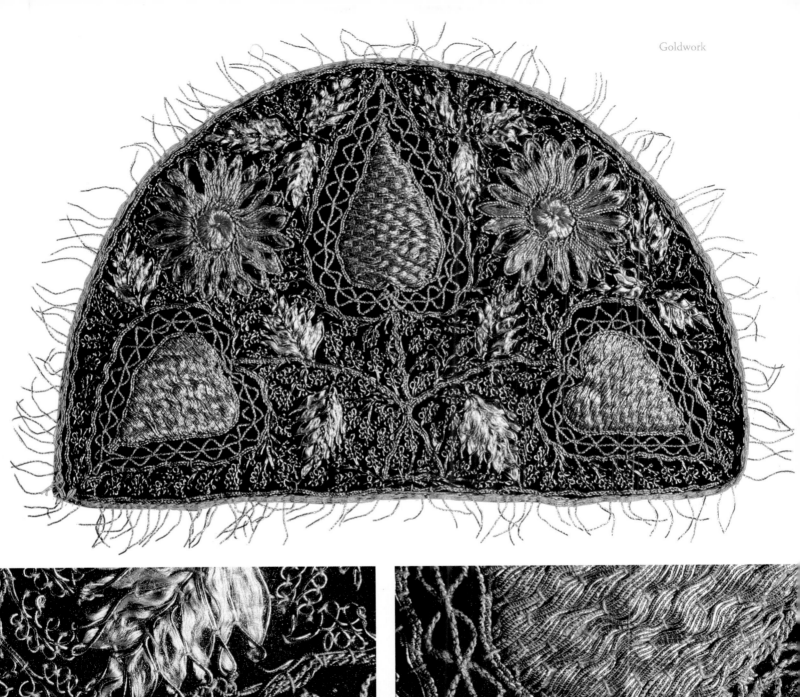

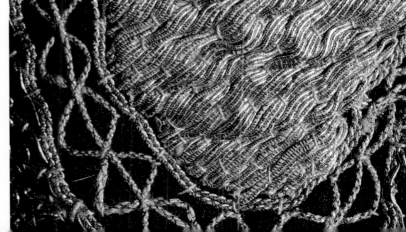

left The heavy, metal thread work on these small, embroidered mats would mean their role was purely decorative. Several different types of purl threads, made by winding gold or silver wire round a thin rod, are included. These wound threads were couched down as a line, or chopped up and sewn like bugle beads. A twisted silver cord fringe is added to all four sides.

Detail 80 x 70mm (3¼ x 2¾in)
India, *c.* 1890

above An evening bag has a peacock design worked onto the front flap. The bird is proudly displaying his tail feathers, which are worked in silver gilt metal threads – check purl and pearl purl – combined with silk floss embroidery in blue and red.

175 x 100mm (7 x 4in)
India, 1960–1970

above This oblong *Chakla* embroidery may have
been used as a festival cloth. A design of three
large sun circles, within a border of semi-circles
and smaller circles, is a good choice for couched
spirals of metal thread. Rope stitch is included,
while Shisha buttonhole stitches hold little mirrors
onto the red cotton background.

350 x 600mm (13¾ x 23½in)
Rajasthan, India, *c.* 1970

right This little bag has been cut from a Sari
fabric. The red, yellow and purple silk material is
embroidered with tambour chain stiches in gold
thread. A fine, metal hook called an *Ari* hook is
used to draw the fine, gold cord from beneath the
work to form a line of chain stitches on top. Flat,
gold sequins are added to outline a pattern of
lapped circles. Two thread tassels decorate the
lower edge.

160 x 200mm (6¼ x 8in)
India, *c.* 1980

above and right A stiffened panel, intended for a bag front, features a peacock with a decorative tail perched on a branch. Metal threads in gold and silver – pearl purl, smooth and check purls – are used to couch the silk embroidery cords. Beads are added for the flower centres and tail. The reverse of the peacock panel shows the construction methods. A stiffened calico is glued behind the black velvet ground, giving a firm foundation for the metal thread embroidery.

200 x 160mm (8 x 6¼in)
Rajasthan, India, 1989

174

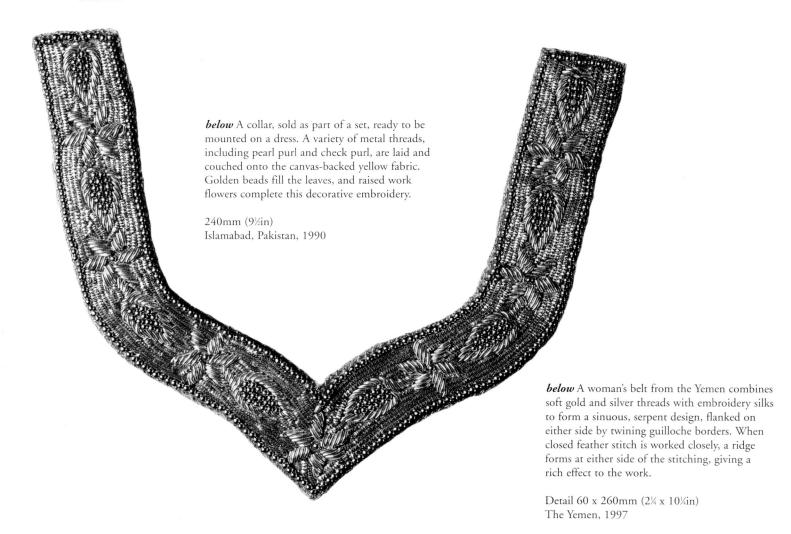

below A collar, sold as part of a set, ready to be mounted on a dress. A variety of metal threads, including pearl purl and check purl, are laid and couched onto the canvas-backed yellow fabric. Golden beads fill the leaves, and raised work flowers complete this decorative embroidery.

240mm (9½in)
Islamabad, Pakistan, 1990

below A woman's belt from the Yemen combines soft gold and silver threads with embroidery silks to form a sinuous, serpent design, flanked on either side by twining guilloche borders. When closed feather stitch is worked closely, a ridge forms at either side of the stitching, giving a rich effect to the work.

Detail 60 x 260mm (2¼ x 10¼in)
The Yemen, 1997

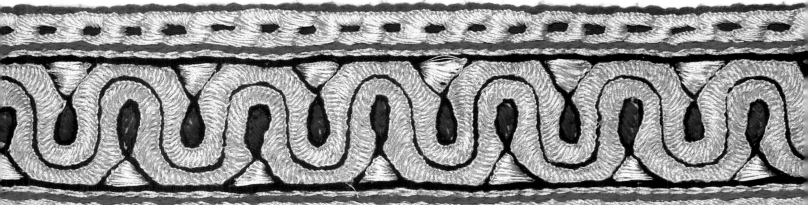

China and Japan

right One of a pair of Civil Rank badges, from the 6th Rank during the Qing period. The Mandarins wore these badges on the front and back of their robes to show their position in the Court hierarchy. Metal thread embroidery is used to depict the egret, together with symbolic motifs – the fan, flower basket, gourd and sacred knot. Double and single gold-covered threads are couched at regular intervals.

Detail 305 x 190mm (12 x 7½in)
China, *c.* 1880

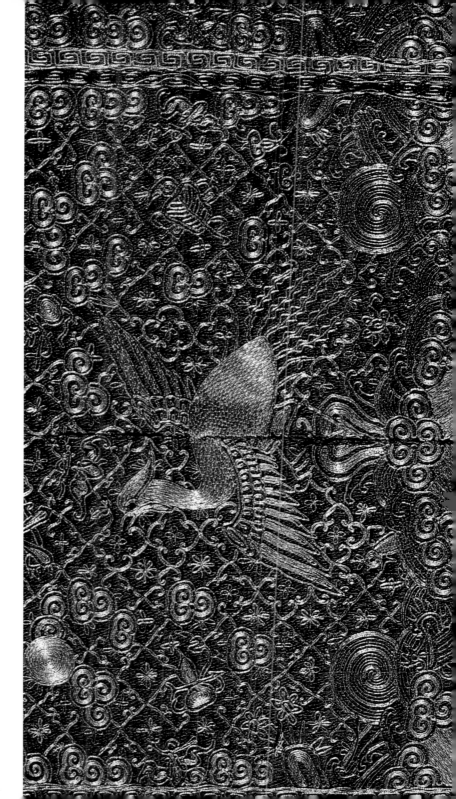

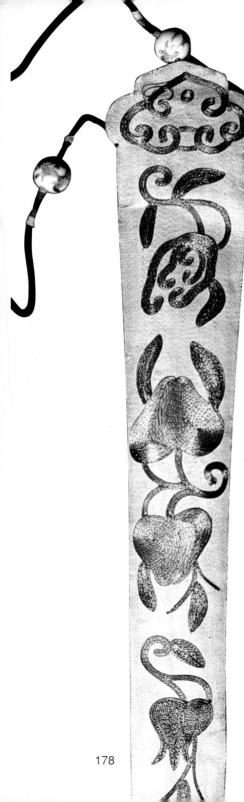

left This stiffened fan case from China is embroidered with metal threads in gold and silver to delineate the flowers and pear-shaped motifs. Closely couched lines of double metal threads are combined with silks in shades of green and mauve. A beaded cord would attach the fan case to the waist belt.

250mm (9¾in)
China, late 19th century

above A *han-eri,* or half collar, was worn by Japanese ladies beneath the outer collar bands of the Kimono. Although only a narrow edge would be visible, they were decorated with exquisite embroidery in silk and golden threads. Faultlessly laid silk cords form satin-stitched flowers and Paulownia leaves, all outlined with finely couched gold thread including the auspicious bow knot.

Detail 155 x 140mm (6¼ x 5½in)
Japan, *c.* 1890

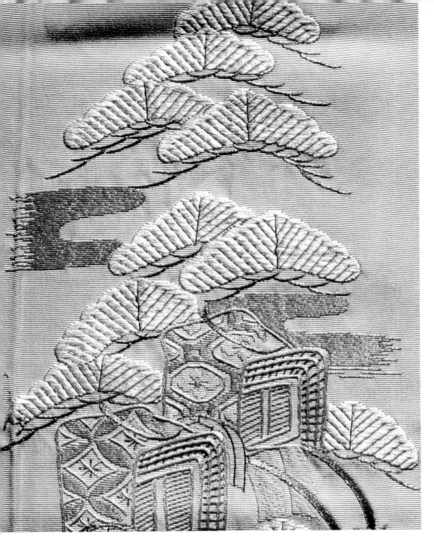

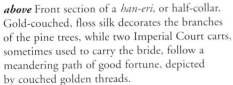

above Front section of a *han-eri*, or half-collar. Gold-couched, floss silk decorates the branches of the pine trees, while two Imperial Court carts, sometimes used to carry the bride, follow a meandering path of good fortune, depicted by couched golden threads.

Detail 155 x 140mm (6¼ x 5½in)
Japan, *c.* 1890

above Front section of a *han-eri*, or half collar. The embroidery design depicts a paper origami version of a crane, a symbol of good luck. The lowers and bamboo sprays are satin-stitched in matt silk, while the crane and the symbolic Paulownia leaves are embroidered in floss silk couched with gold threads.

Detail 155 x 100mm (6¼ x 4in)
Japan, *c.* 1890

left Single lines of gold and silver thread, together with coloured silks, form the encrusted patterns of the central disc motif. This wall panel was possibly cut from a larger piece, and framed with brocade ribbon borders. A design of peacock birds with tails and flowers contrasts with the indigo-dyed silk ground.

360 x 440mm (14¼ x 17¼in)
Guizhou, South-west China, *c.* 1930

left A cut-out motif of a little house, with a lotus-flower inside, may have been used as a good luck token. Double lines of gold-wrapped threads are couched onto a plain, cotton fabric with a red silk thread. The motif is glued onto a thick paper backing that has characters written in black, Chinese ink.

100–150 x 120mm (4–6 x 4¾in)
China, *c.* 1970

right The standard of this gold and silver laid work is very high. Double lines of gold thread are couched with red silk thread, contrasting with the long-and-short satin stitches in shades of floss silk. Embroidery on a square mat includes a bird, lotus flowers and golden thunderline motifs.

200mm sq. (8in sq.)
China, *c.* 1980

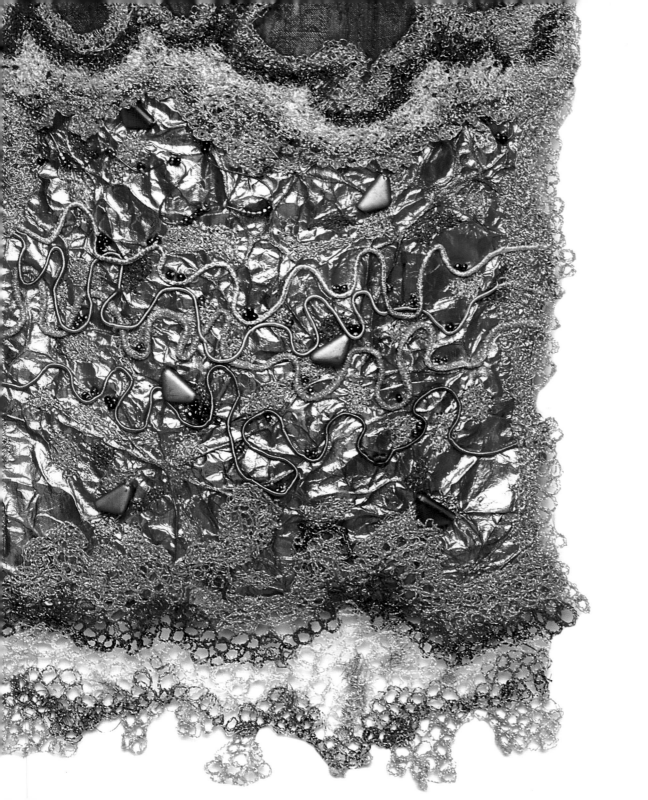

Chapter Six
Machine Embroidery

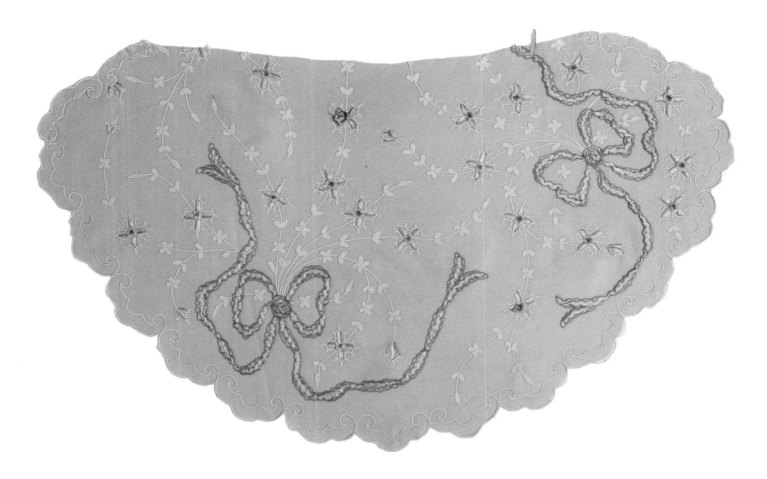

above Sadly, a beautiful evening cape has been cut in half. A beige, wool, face cloth is professionally embroidered in braided ribbon using the Cornely chain-stitch machine. Cords are held down by retard stitch where the chain stitch loops almost cover the applied cord. Some hand-worked ribbon embroidery is added.

390 x 710mm (15½ x 28in)
England or France, *c.* 1905

right This V-shaped collar is probably from a professional workshop. Satin stitch machine embroidery, together with zigzag over cord and the decorative Vermicelli stitch, are machined onto cotton voile. The Vandyke pointed edging reflects the triangles of the inner design.

660 x 70mm (26 x 2¾in)
England, *c.* 1910

left Part of a dress front, decorated with chain stitch embroidery onto fine, black net is a good example of Cornely machine work, probably worked in a fashion studio. The operator guides the machine with a rotating handle, while a hooked needle draws the coloured floss silk threads through to the right side. A metallic cord outlines the floral motifs.

Detail 380 x 265 (15 x 10½in)
England or France, 1920s

above A patriotic pair of French knickers is machine-embroidered in zigzag and satin stitch. On one leg, a sailor waves from his ship surrounded by gulls, on the other side the message 'England Expects.....!!' beneath crossed Union flags completes this lighthearted design in a bleak wartime period when humour was essential.

430 x 660mm (17 x 26in)
England, 1940s

187

below During the early 1970s sewing machines with automatic patterns became readily available. Profiled cams were individually inserted to make these basic patterns. This belt was designed to take advantage of this new facility, with automatic stitches holding down thick and thin cords.

55 x 960mm (2¼ x 37¾in)
England, 1975
(*Angela Thompson*)

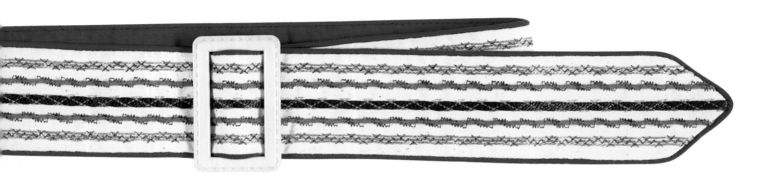

right Free machine embroidery is worked over water-dissolvable fabric. Actual ivy leaves were used as templates for the design. An outlining cord was satin-stitched up and down the stalks and around the leaf shapes in a continuous line. The veins of the leaves and connecting bars were sewn in free straight stitch, joining everything together. Afterwards, the background was dissolved away with hot water.

70–90 x 300mm (2¾–3½ x 11¾in)
England, 1984
(*Angela Thompson*)

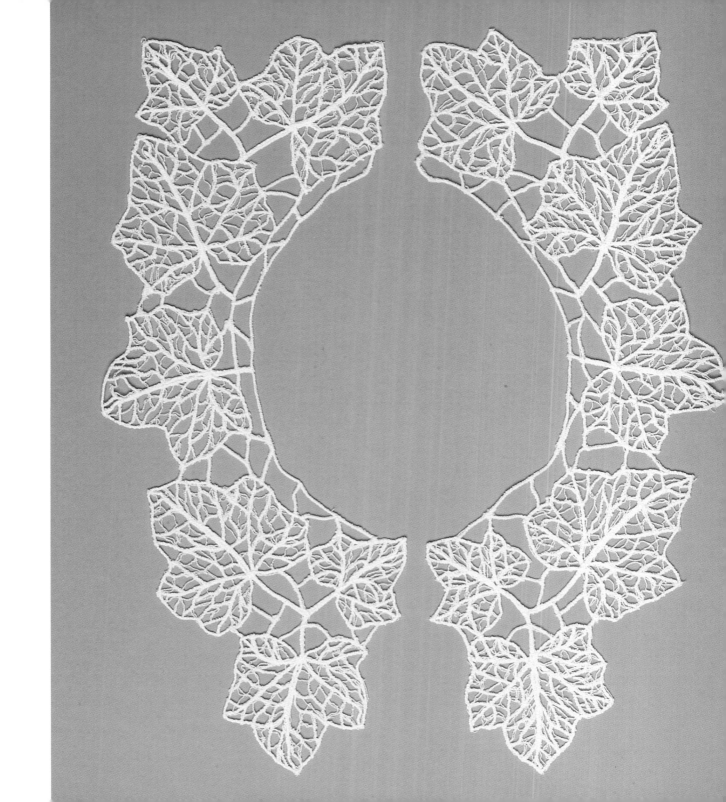

below A greetings card is decorated with diagonal strips of yellow fabric held onto a layer of chiffon, distressed on all four sides. In the centre of the card, a rectangle of chiffon has the inner square cut away to reveal the yellow background, with the inner and outer edges held with straight machine stitches in white thread.

80mm sq. (3¼in sq.)
England, *c.* 1985
(Amanda Clayton)

right A greetings card has a lilac heart applied to pink felt, which is cut away to form an inverted lily, held by close-worked satin stitch. Scrolling lines in free machine stitchery outline the borders and the little Paisley motifs in the corners. Threads are withdrawn from the top and bottom of the piece to form a fringe.

140 x 80mm (5½ x 3¼in)
England, *c.* 1990
(Chloe Walker)

191

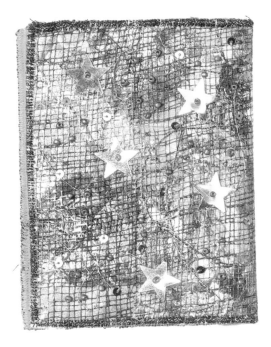

above and right The felt background of these matching needle cases have applied snippets of decorative fabrics and metallic sweet wrappers held with double-sided bonding web. Thicker threads are swirled over, small sequins are scattered and all is topped with a layer of fabric-painted builder's scrim, embroidered with free machine-stitching in swirls using metallic threads. Further beads and sequins are added.

80 x 115mm (3¼ x 4½in)
England, 1999
(*Jane Davies*)

192

left An embroidered triangle has small fabric pieces – braids, lace and broderie anglaise – in white or cream, held to the background using free machine stitchery. The result is dyed with silk and fabric paints, some in gold and bronze. After additional machine embroidery, the whole is mounted onto hot water-dissolvable fabric to add the lacy edging.

75 x 85mm (3¼ x 3½in)
England, *c.* 1988
(*Jane Davies*)

below These machine-embroidered bags were made in a similar way to the embroidered triangle, with the completed work tacked onto hot water-dissolvable fabric to make the lacy edging. When dissolved, a satin stitch outline is machined around the whole piece. Beads and sequins are sewn in place afterwards.

left 80mm sq. (3¼in sq.)
right 90 x 100mm (3½ x 4in)
England, *c.* 1988
(*Jane Davies*)

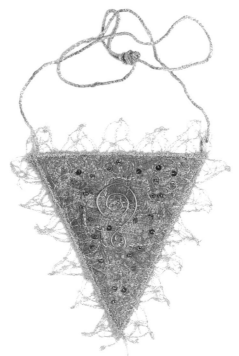

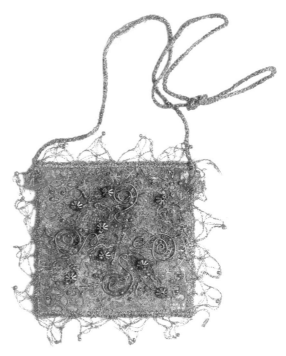

above and right The inner section of this miser's purse is released by the drawstrings. When the extension is pulled out it is possible to see the thin wires couched onto the front surface of the purse by machine and used to support the curves of the lace scallops. Little beads are sewn along the purse top and sides. An interlinked mesh of threads is machine embroidered in a grid formation on to a single layer of cold water-dissolvable fabric. Lacy machine edging, with pendant motifs, is added before dissolving the supporting fabric away.

90 x 180mm (3½ x 7in)
England, 2000
(Dorothy Symmonds)

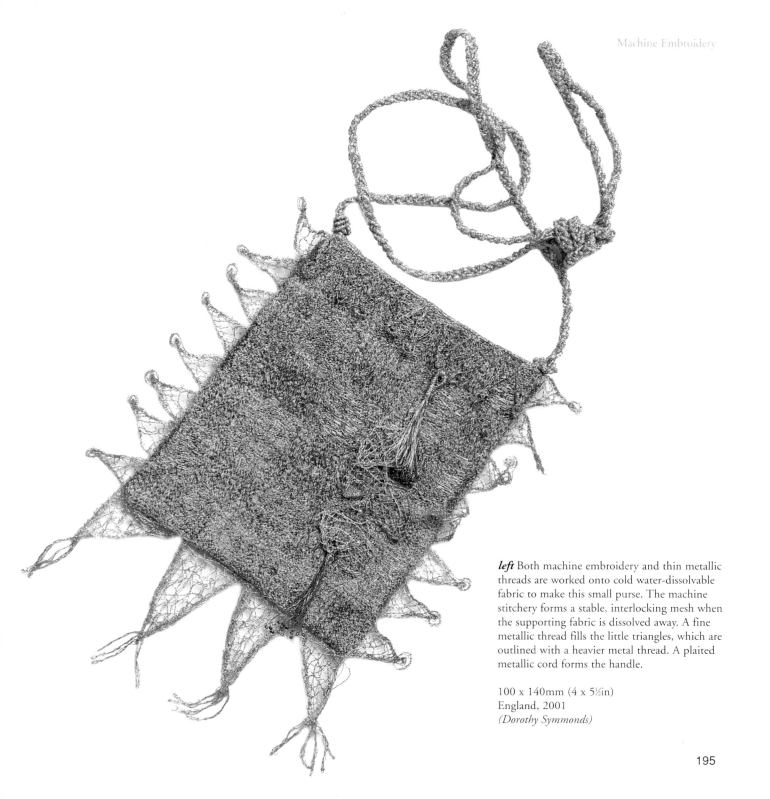

left Both machine embroidery and thin metallic threads are worked onto cold water-dissolvable fabric to make this small purse. The machine stitchery forms a stable, interlocking mesh when the supporting fabric is dissolved away. A fine metallic thread fills the little triangles, which are outlined with a heavier metal thread. A plaited metallic cord forms the handle.

100 x 140mm (4 x 5½in)
England, 2001
(Dorothy Symmonds)

195

left Tyvec fabric – coloured with pearlized paint and then heat-treated – is applied to the background of a little bag. Machine embroidery is added, including machine-wrapped wire. A lacy edging is worked separately onto cold, water-dissolvable fabric, then applied to the top, bottom and sides of the bag. The handle is made of machine-wrapped wire.

110 x 165mm (4¼ x 6½in)
England, 2001
(Dorothy Symmonds)

left and below An embroidered bowl is constructed by using a straight-stitch sewing machine to apply a mesh of closely worked threads onto two layers of cold, water-dissolvable fabric. The stitchery is built up until a viable fabric is formed, then the supporting fabric is dissolved away and the bowl is shaped while still damp. The coloured threads contrast with and outline areas of the interior design, while thicker threads are machine-couched to decorate the rim.

Diameter 200mm (8in)
England, 2003
(Bronwen Jenkins)

197

left Painted and stitched fabric is applied to the silk background of this machine-embroidered bag. Heavy cords are machine-couched around the design outlines of the curved motifs, which are then machine-quilted. A machine-wrapped cord forms the looped border added at the bottom, as well as the handles and knotted ends.

100 x 180mm (4 x 7in)
England, 2003
(Catherine Craig)

right The petalled top of this small container is decorated with little brass bells. Dyed fabric is bonded to heavy-duty interfacing for the separate panels. A computer design is printed onto tissue paper, which is padded with felt before bonding onto the dyed fabric. Free machine-quilting is worked through the layers and finally the panels are stitched together.

70 x 140mm (2¾ x 5½in)
England, 2003
(Marie Roper)

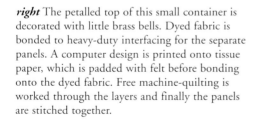

198

left The computer-generated design for this pyramid purse is printed onto tissue, then bonded to the silk background fabric. This is placed over a fine wadding and freely machine-quilted through the layers to outline the pattern motifs. A small zip is inserted for the opening and the sides and tassels decorated with little beads.

100mm (4in)
England, 2004
(Marie Roper)

Chapter Seven
Patchwork

left and above An unfinished patchwork coverlet
uses diamond shapes that, when joined together,
form a tumbling blocks design. A dog-tooth
pattern of elongated triangles is added to make
the border. An eclectic selection of woven silks,
possibly cut from ribbons, forms a rich mosaic
of varied patterns, while the underside of the
coverlet shows the paper templates still tacked
into position. Old letters have been used, several
showing the practice of crossing. To save paper,
the letter was written one way, then the paper
was turned 90 degrees and written the other way.

Detail 100 x 70mm (4 x 2⅜in)
England, *c.* 1860
(Diana Banks Collection)

right Double rosettes of hexagon shapes are combined to create the pattern that is known as Grandmother's Flower Garden. This large, double-bed sized patchwork coverlet was made by Jane Bate-Hughes. Before her marriage in 1861, Jane worked for a dressmaker at Queen Victoria's Court and later set up her own business in the Midlands. The woven silk fabrics used for the coverlet could be from leftover dressmaking scraps.

left The hexagon shapes have been cleverly cut to form new patterns. As an unmarried lady, for propriety's sake, Jane called herself 'Madame Rubery' and made trips to Paris to purchase fabrics. She gave up her business when she married John Hughes, ten years her junior.

Detail 200 x 165mm (8 x 6½in)
England, *c.* 1865

above and right A patchwork coverlet of diamond
shapes cut from printed, cotton fabrics has never
been completed. The diversity of pattern forms a
historical record of fabric prints that may have
taken several years to collect. The detail shows the
papers still in place, some cut from printed matter.
One from an envelope has a postmark 'Haywards
Heath, Oct 14, 87', giving us a definite date after
which the coverlet was assembled.

Detail 170 x 115mm (6¾ x 4½in)
England, *c.* 1887

above A crazy patchwork shelf pelmet or
lambrequin has random-shaped patches in velvet,
silk and satin applied to the background. Orange,
pink and green embroidery silks outline the
patches using herringbone, feather, buttonhole,
stem and satin stitches. Embroidered flowers and
buds are added.

210 x 380mm (8¼ x 15in)
England, *c.* 1880–1890

left Herringbone stitchery is used to hold random-shaped patches onto the background of this crazy cushion cover. Yellow silk embroidery threads contrast with the plain and patterned silks. During this period, silk was treated with a tin-solution to stiffen dress fabrics. This treatment has resulted in deterioration and cracking, a common problem as seen on the green silk frill.

380mm sq. (15in sq.)
England, *c.* 1885–1895

below Two bands of crazy patchwork may have been cut from a larger piece, to use as borders or possibly as a bell-pull as they are seamed to a brown-satin lining fabric. Embroidery stitches hold the random patches, but the silk is now in poor condition.

130 x 510mm (5 x 20in)
England, *c.* 1890–1900

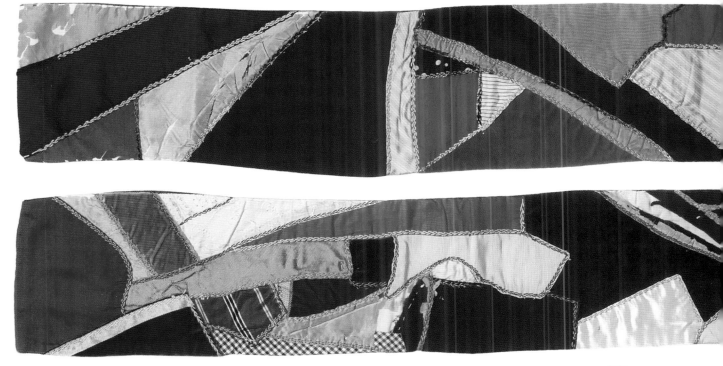

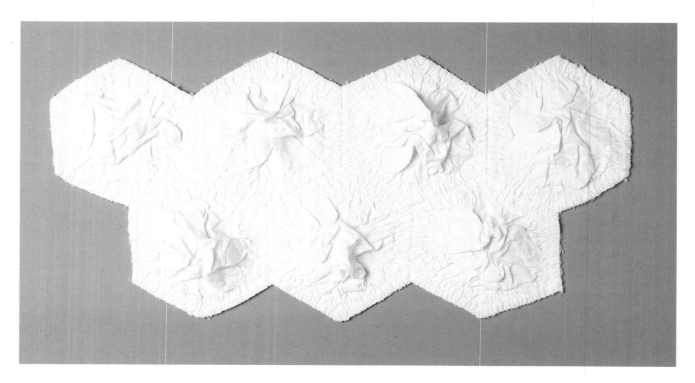

above A section of white puff patchwork has been
removed from a coverlet. Pairs of hexagon shapes
are cut out, one is 50mm (2in) larger than the
other. Lines of gathering stitches are sewn round
the larger hexagon, the threads are drawn up to
fit the smaller hexagon. The two are oversewn
together and the puffs held down by five tie
stitches in the middle.

Hexagon 50mm (2in)
England, 1895–1905
(Daisy Stonehouse)

above This pink cot quilt is made in a version of
log cabin patchwork. The courthouse steps pattern
is made of alternating strips of pink and white
cotton, diminishing in size with each round.
There are fifteen blocks measuring 150 x 125mm
(6 x 5in) quilted with hand run stitches to a white
backing. Quilt patterns include flowers, circles and
shell spirals.

630 x 760mm (24¾ x 30in)
England, *c.* 1910

left A rosebud motif is divided into geometric segments and interpreted as patchwork inlay in coloured suede. Design points are emphasized with straight stitches in thin metallic thread, taken through to the background.

200mm sq. (8in sq.)
England, 1976
(*Angela Thompson*)

right Folded star patchwork made from stiffened fabric or ribbons is arranged to form a design of triangles, overlapping each successive round. Oblongs are folded in half widthways, then mitred to form a triangular point. The triangular pieces are stitched from the centre, with the raw edges covered by the following row.

Diameter 90mm (3½in)
England, *c.* 1990
(*Jane Rawlins*)

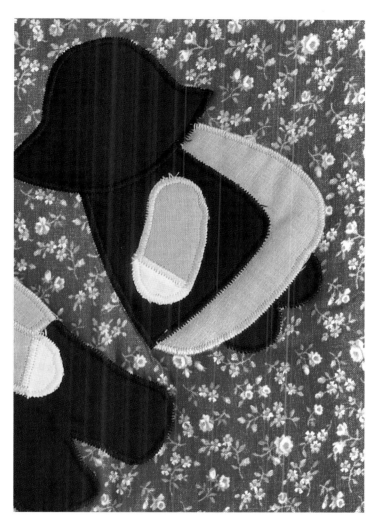

above and right The Amish from Pennsylvania do
not believe in showing people's faces, so these little
dolls have blank faces and the boy and girl on this
pot holder hide beneath their black felt hats. Plain
fabrics are applied to a printed background and
stitched through the layers to form a pad.

180 x 165mm (7 x 6½in)
USA, 1995

above and right The machine-pieced pattern for
this miniature quilt is based on blocks of crazy
patchwork that form an inner border, placed
within a square. Free machine embroidery and
quilting decorates the inner corners and the dyed
fabric of the outer borders. A mono-printed fabric
is used for the binding.

610mm sq. (24in sq.)
England, 1999
(*Marie Roper*)

above and left No formal pattern shapes were
used for the freely cut pieces that are joined to
make this quilted, patchwork picture. Both hand-
dyed and commercial fabrics form the basis of the
design which features hand- and machine-quilting
with the addition of shaped, turquoise beads. A
narrow, hand-dyed binding is added on all four
sides of the piece.

360mm sq. (14⅛in sq.)
England, 2002
(*Marie Roper*)

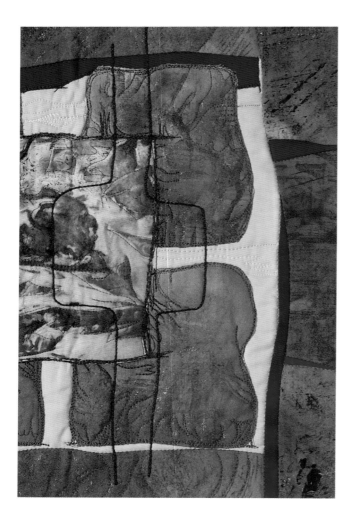

above and left Five Rocks is the descriptive name
given to this pieced quilt. The five squares, which
are made from mono-printed and hand-painted
fabrics, are bonded to the background fabric. Free
machine-quilting lines suggest the textured areas
of the rocks and machine-couched cords define
the design outlines.

380mm sq. (15in sq.)
England, 2000
(*Marie Roper*)

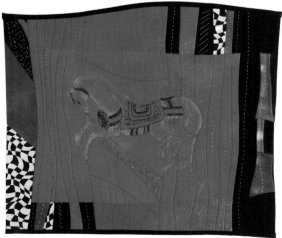

above and left Machine-embroidery decorates the stencilled horse that is the focal point of this pictorial patchwork hanging. A variety of plain and patterned fabric pieces are cut freely and pieced to make the outer borders, while both hand- and machine-quilting give emphasis to the design.

460 x 410mm (18 x 16¼in)
England, 2002
(Marie Roper)

217

Chapter Eight

Quilting and Padded Work

above and left This furnishing fragment is
probably cut from a bed curtain, later made into
a chair seat. The design shows acanthus leaves,
flowers and trailing stems, embroidered through
three fabric layers with couching, satin, stem, chain
and speckling stitches, together with French knots
and bullion knots. Embroidery threads are silk
and linen on linen fabric with a coarser backing.

590 x 230mm (23½ x 9in)
England, *c.* 1705–1710

above and right Corded quilting is worked
through two layers of linen, the top fine, the
backing coarse, on this superb fragment cut from
a bed coverlet. Intertwined double lines of quilted
back stitch form the narrow channels, which are
later threaded with quilting wool from behind.
Meandering lines and linked circles are flat-quilted
through two fabric layers for the background
design, using cream silk thread.

320 x 260mm (12½ x 10¼in)
England, *c.* 1710–1720

221

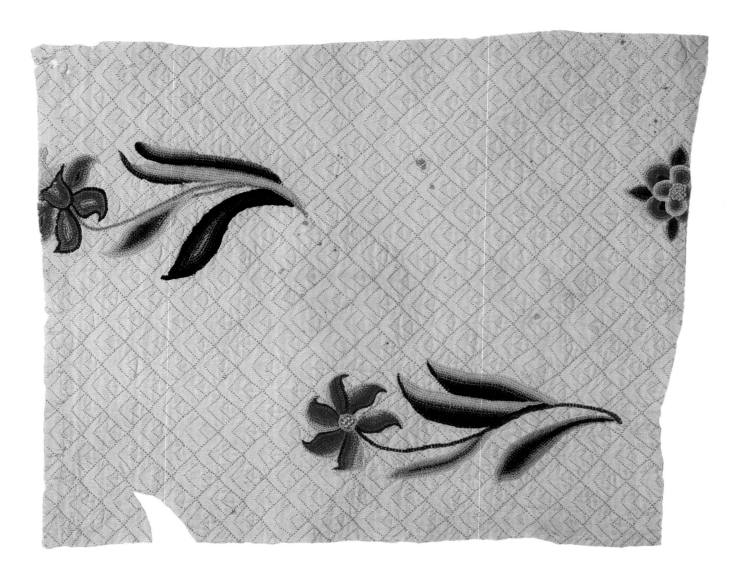

above Linen fabric mounted on a scrim backing forms the basis for the wool and silk embroidery and quilting of a bed-hanging piece. Chain stitching on the back reverses on the right side to quilting lines, possibly worked with a tambour hook. Shaded floral motifs, set within the diaper quilted ground, contain chain stiches, threaded cross and bullion knots.

200 x 250mm (8 x 9⅞in)
India, *c.* 1750

below Back-stitching through two layers of cotton fabric forms the flat-quilted, diamond pattern on a fragment of Mughal Indian embroidery. A repeat design of ogees outlined with metal thread would at one time cover the fabric surface. A flower with two buds is worked in shaded long-and-short stitch, satin and couching using silk threads.

180 x 110mm (7 x 4¼in)
India, *c.* 1780

above and right The design of heavily padded fruit on this black tea cosy is typical of the Art Deco period after World War I. The leaves are stiffened with wire, while a covered wire curves to join the two padded motifs together. Similar colours and shapes are illustrated as embroidery patterns in women's magazines of the time.

310 x 210mm (12½ x 8¼in)
England, *c.* 1910–1920

above and left A linen nightdress case has a design of flower medallions encircled with geometric interlacing, worked in Italian quilting on two layers of fabric. Narrow channels outlined with backstitching are threaded from behind with quilting wool to form padded ridges and petal forms. Made for her sister's birthday by Margaret Hamer on 3rd September, when World War II was declared on the radio.

390 x 320mm (15¼ x 12½in)
England, 1939

225

above Backstitch quilting in silk thread forms
the background grid of diagonal lines on this
silk nightdress case. The formal flower sprays
inside the cross medallions are embroidered with
chain, buttonhole, feather, Cretan, Romanian and
needlelace filling stitches. This is another precisely
dated example of superior craftsmanship.

390 x 320mm (15¼ x 12½in)
England, 1941
(Margaret Hamer)

226

left and below A chakla square is folded to make an envelope bag, embroidered through two fabric layers with double-run step stitch, to form a quilted diaper pattern on the borders. The nomadic Banjara people also decorated their carrying bags with thread pompoms, couched threads and shisha mirror glass.

330mm sq. (13in sq.)
North-west India, 1965

left Kantha, meaning cloth, is the name given to quilting through three layers of cotton fabric, worked by the women of Bangladesh during the rainy season. Rows of fine running stitches surround a traditional 100-petal lotus flower motif worked in pattern darning, together with leaf sprays and buds. Cloths were used for cushions, covers and wall hangings.

Detail 200 x 230mm (8 x 9in)
Bangladesh, *c.* 1985

right and below A Kantha quilt sample in progress, showing three cloth layers tacked together. Stem outline stitching and pattern darning are used for the central lotus flower and bud motif. Finely worked quilt running stitches follow the contours of the motifs to form a firm but supple fabric. Kantha motifs expressed the wish for good luck, fruitful harvests or, for weddings, symbols of plenty and fertility. Traditionally this is a thrift craft that uses coloured threads that have been withdrawn from old saris.

180mm sq. (7in sq.)
Bangladesh, 1987
(Bangladesh Exhibition, London)

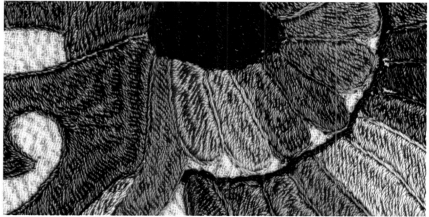

above and right Co-operative workshops were
set up in Bangladesh as a sale outlet for Kantha
quilting on cushion covers and cloths. Women
followed set designs, but interpreted them
individually. Quilt running, pattern darning,
stem stitches and couching depict a whimsical
scene, including a mother and baby elephant.

410mm sq. (16¼in sq.)
Bangladesh, *c.* 1988

left and below A mirrored design of two elephants, each with a bird standing on its back, is finely quilted in Kantha darning stitch to both fill and surround the motifs. Contrasting lines of stem stitch in pale blue outline the various pattern elements. The embroidery forms the front of a little cushion.

240mm sq. (9½in sq.)
Bangladesh, *c.* 1990

231

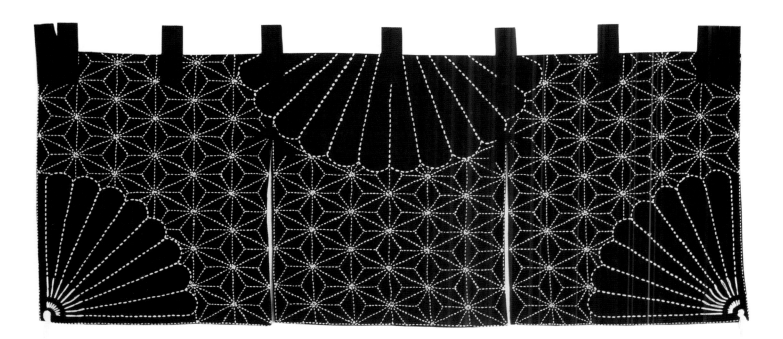

left Japanese Sashiko quilting originated as
a practical craft where farmers, firemen and
other manual workers needed warm, serviceable
clothing. Their wives would sew two layers of
indigo-dyed cotton cloth together in contrasting
white thread. Gradually, patterns became more
stylized, and this circular mat shows the
traditional hemp leaf motif.

Diameter 200mm (8in)
Takayama, Japan, 1994

above A Sashiko-quilted door hanging is in three
parts, joined at the top with loops for a rod. A
fan pattern is repeated at the corners, embellished
with thread tassels. The ancient hemp leaf pattern
fills in the ground. This is said to represent the
power of the Buddha, which radiates like light
from the central spokes of each motif.

760 x 410mm (30 x 16¼in)
Takayama, Japan, 1994

below Silk fabric dyes, fixed by ironing, are painted onto thin Japanese silk that has been stretched onto a frame. Colours are allowed to run, forming the flower and leaf shapes. The flower centres and leaf veins are freely machine-quilted onto a synthetic wadding with one quilted leaf cut out and applied. Beads and bugles are added.

410 x 310mm (16¼ x 12½in)
England, 1994
(Angela Thompson)

right The flower and leaf motifs of this little silk purse are painted onto the background with silk dye, then machine quilted round the design outlines. The flower petals are painted separately, machine-quilted and then cut out before applying in diminishing layers to the main flower. A hand-twisted cord is made from a hank of stranded embroidery thread.

140 x 110mm (5½ x 4¼in)
England, 1995
(Angela Thompson)

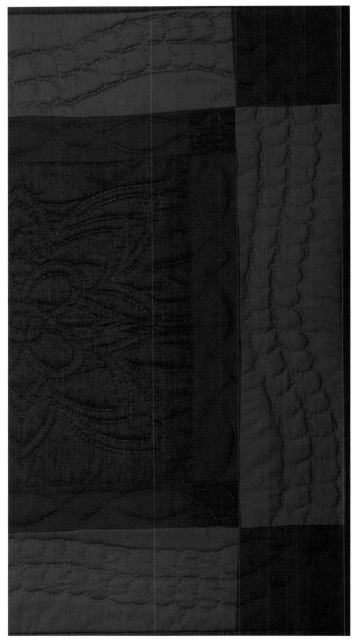

above and right The Amish women, in keeping with their religious principles, are conservative in their dress but find artistic expression in patchwork and quilting. They always use plain fabrics, but colours such as the purple and green of this small quilt, sing when joined together. The hand-run quilting which takes the form of a central flower medallion with border wave patterns, is worked on a standing quilt frame.

685mm sq. (27in sq.)
Bird-in-Hand, Pennsylvania, USA 1997

below A round hat made from grey, acrylic fleece, has applied motifs in red, yellow and blue cut through as reverse appliqué. All the layers are embroidered with machine-stitching, both to outline and enhance the appliqué motifs and decorate the crown surface and padded brim.

Diameter 190mm (7½in)
England, 2003
(Bronwen Jenkins)

right An innovative, three-dimensional interpretation of the traditional quilt, worked in a striking and unusual leaf design. The background fabric was hand-dyed to make this leafy wall hanging, then a variety of leaf shapes were printed onto the dyed fabric. The individual leaves were created from dyed fabric, placed on a layer of padding and ground fabric, freely machine-embroidered and cut out to form three-dimensional shapes. Machine-wrapped cord forms the twining stems.

400 x 760mm (15¾ x 30in)
England, 2003
(*Bronwen Jenkins*)

238

below Three-dimensional boxes inspired by Charles Dickens' Victorian novel *Great Expectations*. Machine embroidery was used for each Jack-in-the-box. In one, the padded, wire figure of Abel Magwitch is the Jack, with the panels depicting the Kent marshes. The other shows Miss Havisham, with the machine-embroidered panels on the box following the descriptions of her apartments, including the fireplace where her bridal dress caught fire.

75mm sq. (3in sq.)
England, 2003
(Lorna Pound)

239

below Green and purple acrylic fabrics were
used to make this child's round hat with a crown-
shaped upturned brim. Layers are quilted through
with free embroidery, using the straight stitch
machine to outline the applied motifs. The quilted
crown is finished with a padded, bobble knob
with embroidered tassels.

Diameter 130mm (5in)
England, 2004
(*Catherine Craig*)

above The designs for this small stand, taken from 12th-century tiles in Afghanistan, are worked in corded quilting. The hexagon shape of the lidded stand is formed from six panels, each one painted and further embellished with irregular cross-stitches to simulate the iridescent surface where the glaze on the ancient tiles had deteriorated.

100 x 110mm (4 x 4¼in)
England, 2004
(Lorna Pound)

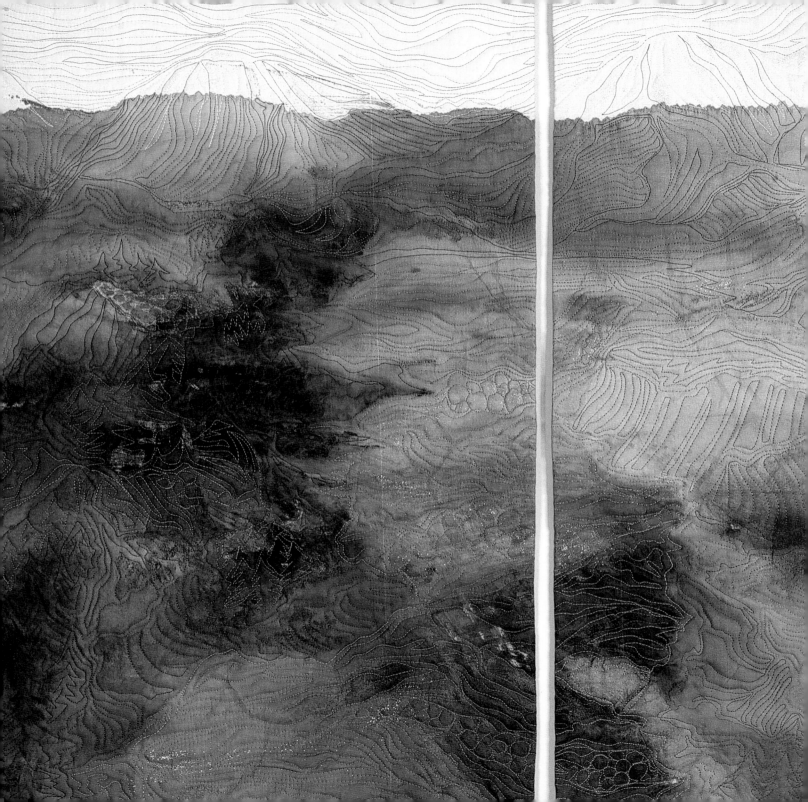

left The topographical quality of *Winter Mist* is enhanced by the use of free machine-quilting on the acrylic painted, cotton background fabric. The addition of iridescent paint adds further to the luminous feeling of the mist as it softly encroaches and recedes within the landscape.

1000mm sq. (39¼in sq.)
England, 2001
(Sandra Meech)

right *Shoofly* is the name given to this contemporary quilt. The survival of the Inuit hunters in the harsh Arctic climate depended on the sewing skill of their womenfolk, which enabled them to produce well-made caribou-skin clothing. This quilt is a celebration of these women and their generations of needlework expertise. Both printed transfer images and acrylic paintings depict the subject matter on the machine pieced, quilted, dye printed background fabric.

1000 x 1700mm (39¼ x 67in)
England, 2001
(Sandra Meech, Collection of the Museum of Art and Design, New York)

above Comet-tailed stars streak across the quilted sky of *Starry, Starry Night*. A repeat pattern of spiky star shapes is outlined with metallic threads machined onto a printed transfer background. Decorative lurex nets form the comet tails and the starry firmament, while the padding of trapunto and stitched quilting adds a three-dimensional quality to the work.

254 x 203mm (10 x 8in)
England, 1994
(*Sandra Meech*)

right A diary quilt, entitled *Five Days in May: Pages from an Arctic Journal*, records the thoughts, photographs and memories of time spent with the Inuit people of northern Canada. The areas of Baker Lake and Rankin Inlet were the inspiration for this series of five diary strips showing Rock, Ice, Skin, Hamlet and Tundra as an evocative sequence of pictorial scenes and calligraphic records.

1600m sq. (63in sq.)
England, 2000
(*Sandra Meech*)

245

above and left In *Northern Reflections*, a pictorial journey takes us through the Arctic tundra to explore the lives of the Inuit people and gain an understanding of their relationship with a harsh environment. Interlinked rectangles both contain and expand upon a variety of elements, including descriptive scenes of hunting, fishing, sledging, bird and animal life. Appliqué shapes on the centre blocks and on the outside borders are held with bonding web, with additional satin stitch embroidery and hand quilting.

1524mm sq. (60in sq)
England, 1995
(Sandra Meech)

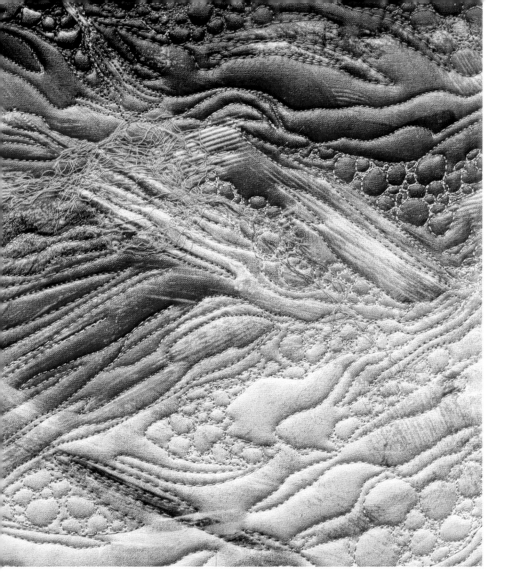

left and above Acrylic paint on cotton is used to create this beautiful quilt. Called *Towards the Sun*, the quilt has been freely machine-quilted to reflect the golden colours of the Arctic spring.

127 x 203 mm (5 x 8in)
England, 2002
(Sandra Meech)

Chapter Nine
Smocking

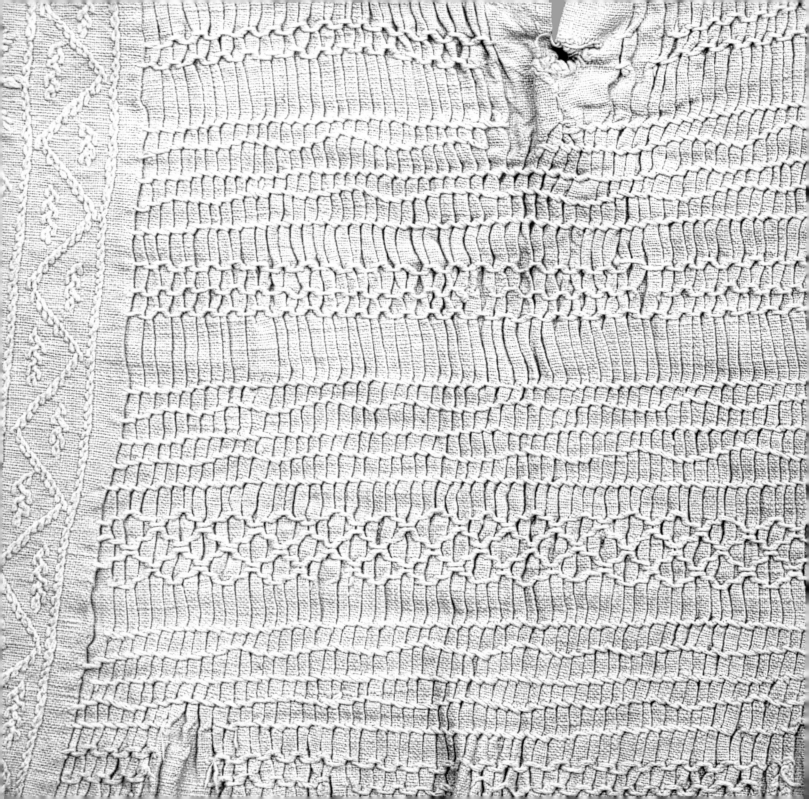

left Section of a round smock showing the front neck slit, smocked front and embroidered side-boxes. By the mid-19th century the working smock had become more decorative, and was often reserved for Sundays or for best wear. Smocking stitches include cable, trellis and rope or outline. The side-boxes are worked in a very close single-feather stitch.

Detail 175 x 200mm (7 x 8in)
England, 1850–1860

right A child's blue, cotton, smocked coat, with a cape collar, has a front opening fastened with mother-of-pearl buttons. The cape collar has spirals, trees and chevrons embroidered with feather, chain and herringbone stitches. Rope, cable, Vandyke and trellis smocking stitches are worked on the front and sleeves. Upper class children were dressed in these versions of adult working clothes as a relaxation from formal dress.

445 x 240mm (17½ x 9½in)
England, 1880–1900
(Worcestershire County Museum)

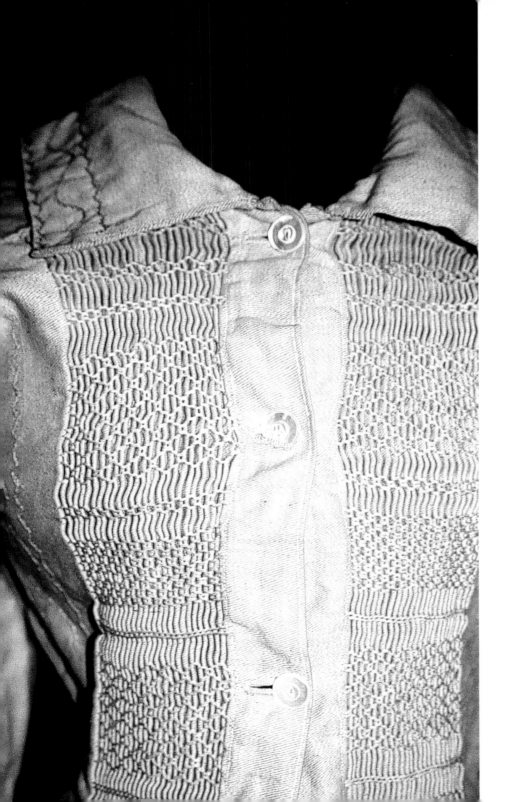

left A woman's machine-sewn coat of Holland linen, shaped to the waist and fastened with mother-of-pearl buttons. The collar, yoke and cuffs are hand-embroidered. The side-boxes are hand-stitched with alternating zigzags and meanders in single-feather. Smocking stitches include, trellis, cable and diamond. This is not a working smock, but part of a late 19th-century aesthetic fashion for rural crafts.

Detail 445 x 240mm (17½ x 9½in)
England, 1890–1910
(Worcestershire County Museum)

right A detail showing the front, collar and cuff sections of a Worcestershire coat smock, embroidered by the last female smock maker in the town of Bewdley on the River Severn. Identical smocks were made for the author's grandfather and grandmother, but it is doubtful that they ever wore them. The tear-drop motifs and zigzags on the shoulder of the smock are worked in chain stitch.

410 x 380mm (16¼ x 15in)
England, 1898

left A front view of Grandfather Herbert Stonehouse's coat smock, showing the smocking reeds, or gathers, on the cuff and at the base of the smocked panels on the front opening. Stitches include rope, cable and trellis. A ladder of chain and detached chain stitch motifs are worked up both sides of the smocked front panels.

Detail 510 x 310mm (20 x 12⅛in)
England, 1898

right The back view of a ladies' smock made for Daisy Stonehouse. It is fashionably fitted to the waist and upper body, unlike the man's looser smock. The large shoulder capes, which were placed beneath the small round collar, were worn by shepherds on the hills, as the double cloth gave extra protection from the rain.

380 x 1420mm (15 x 56in)
England, 1898

left and above A child's smock in blue linen, probably made for a little boy, is hand stitched throughout. A light and a dark blue, soft cotton thread contrasts with the background fabric. Rows of triple feather stitch in pale blue outline the collar and cuff borders, while stem stitch is used for the interlocking Greek key lines on either side. The neck opening is at the back, with similar smocked panels on either side. Smocking stitches include rope, trellis, cable, Vandyke and feather.

380 x 520mm (15 x 20½in)
England, 1909–1912

below Smocking stitches in coloured embroidery silks are used to decorate the front panels of a child's smock made in olive green shantung silk. Stitches include, rope, cable, wave and honeycomb. The fabric-covered buttons and the embroidered collar are representative of the folk embroidery revival and establishment of cottage industries.

Detail 330 x 210 (13 x 8¼in)
England, *c.* 1910–1920

Chapter Ten

Tassels and Fringes

right A Berlin work bag is embroidered in cross stitch on double thread canvas, in a block and line pattern using silk and wool threads. A multi-coloured cord forms the handles and outlines the edges of the bag. The sides are embellished with groups of twisted, chenille-thread tassels, each ending with a little wrapped-thread ball.

140 x 110mm (5½ x 4¼in)
England, 1820–1830

right The vertical stripes on this Berlin work bag are embroidered in Hungarian stitch onto double thread canvas, using silk and woollen threads. The bag is edged with a twisted silk cord, which also forms the handles. The same silk is used to make the decorative ends of the tassels, which hang on either side of the open-topped bag. Wrapped silk threads and needlelace stitches cover the tassel heads.

160 x 170mm (6¼ x 6⅜in)
England, 1825–1835

above The town of Casalguidi, in northern Italy, is home to this convent-inspired embroidery, later taken up as a pastime in England. A four-sided stitch grid is the basis for raised embroidery on linen. Tassel heads are covered with needlelace stitches. A length of cord is knotted twice at spaced intervals, then chopped up to make the tied, knotted groups that form the tassels ends.

170 x 210mm (6¾ x 8½in)
England, 1905–1910

far left Wrapped cords with strung beads, Turk's head knots and metal beads decorate these Uzbek hair tassels. They are worn with a pair hanging down each side of the headdress. The tassels are formed of twisted double silk threads and hang down in layers.

640mm (25¼in)
Uzbekistan, 1950–1960

left These hair tassels, which elongate the plaits and hang below the veil, are decorated with spiral bead and thread wrapping above the tassels. They have a core of thread, which is covered with detached buttonhole stitches. Three beaded braids are divided to form six beaded tassels with extra beads sewn onto the tassels ends.

850mm (33½in)
Nuristan, East Afghanistan, 1950–1960

above A border of elaborate tassels is attached to the network edging on this Uzbeki bedding wrap. As nomadic people have little use for furniture in their tents, cloths were used to cover the pile of folded bed covers during the day. The beaded tassels would hang down to form both a useful and a decorative function.

250 x 940mm (9¾ x 37in)
Uzbekistan, *c.* 1955–1960

above Folded loops of black threads are suspended from netting. The shanks are decorated with small beads, wrapped in a close spiral above plaited Turk's head knots. Many shanks include a larger, silver-coloured metal bead. Below, the tied, black tassels are covered with purple braid folded to form a flower-calyx shape. Tiny crystal beads are added to the tassel thread ends.

360mm (14¼in)
Uzbekistan, *c.* 1955–1960

below Approximately 30 tassels, beaded and wrapped in thread, are sewn at intervals onto both sides of a red velvet bag from Bokhara. More are also added on the draw-strings. Thread colours are yellow, pink, black, white, red, purple and green. Small crystal beads are sewn to the tassel ends and a larger bead is inserted on the tassel head.

160 x 190mm (6¼ x 7½in)
Uzbekistan, *c.* 1950–1960

above An ornamental hanging has been cut from an embroidered *Suzani,* which is made from four separate panels, with the joins displacing the floral motifs. A curved border, together with network and rows of decorative thread tassels, has been added, possibly in the early 20th century.

690 x 1140mm (27¼ x 45in)
Uzbekistan, late 19th century
(Decorative Arts Museum, Tashkent)

left Round beads are sewn in clusters to decorate a woman's dress front. Sun-ray pattern motifs, embroidered in square chain stitches, form the background of this square. Circular beadwork medallions called *gul-i-peron*, meaning dress flowers, are attached to the embroidered surface, defining the cross shape of the design. Beads are sewn round the central bead through thick layers of cloth to make these medallions. A cord fringe of bead clusters is sewn round the central *gul* and along the four outer borders.

260mm sq. (10¼in sq.)
Afghanistan, 1965–1970

right Geometric bands of diamonds, squares and lozenges are embroidered in cross stitch onto the front of an open-topped bag using cotton thread. A fringe of twisted cotton cord decorates the three closed sides. Round, white beads are threaded onto the fringe-loop ends.

120 x 140mm (4¾ x 5½in)
Baluchistan, 1965–1970

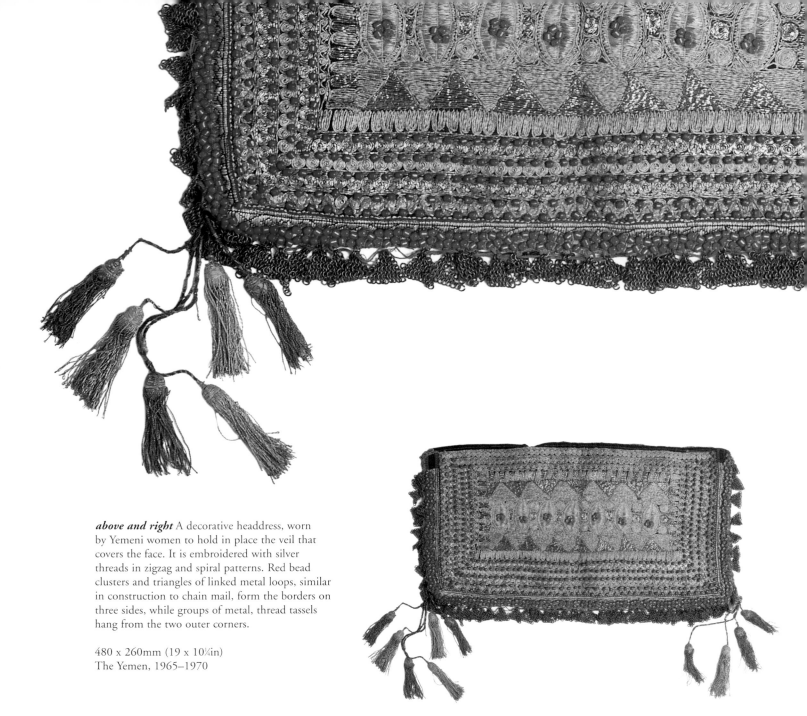

above and right A decorative headdress, worn
by Yemeni women to hold in place the veil that
covers the face. It is embroidered with silver
threads in zigzag and spiral patterns. Red bead
clusters and triangles of linked metal loops, similar
in construction to chain mail, form the borders on
three sides, while groups of metal, thread tassels
hang from the two outer corners.

480 x 260mm (19 x 10¼in)
The Yemen, 1965–1970

left Cotton and metal threads are used to wrap the divided strands of this netted hair decoration. Wrapped, cord pairs are tied with wrapped-thread knots before they are divided to re-join with tassels and end with bunched floss thread tassels and metal discs.

230mm (9in)
Sind, Pakistan, 1975–1980

far left Three cotton-thread cords are embellished with buttons and beaded tassels that hang down in layered groups to make this heavily decorated hair tassel. Cowrie shells are added to the bead clusters and tassel tops.

790mm (31in)
Nuristan, Afghanistan, 1975–1980

271

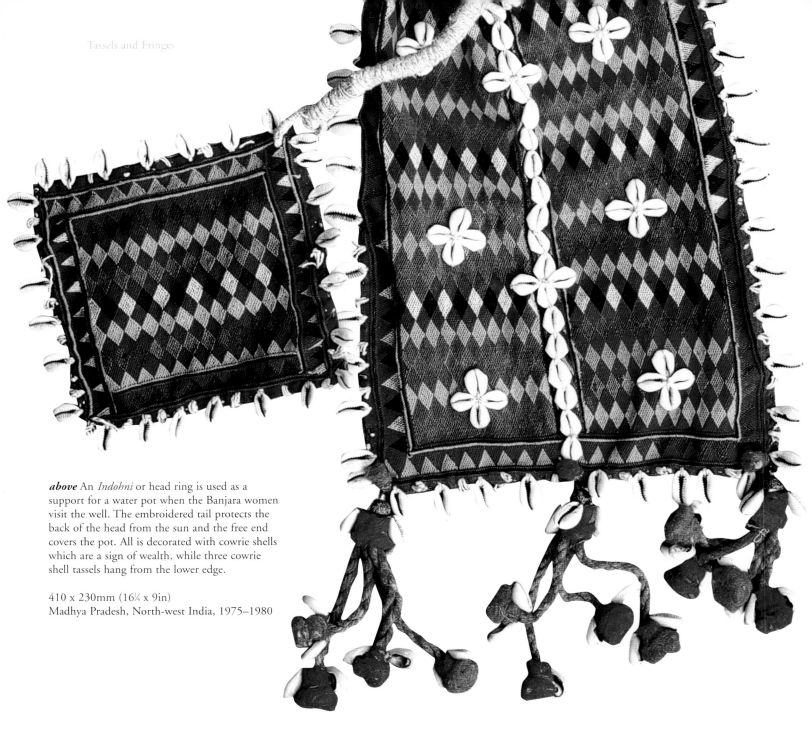

above An *Indohni* or head ring is used as a support for a water pot when the Banjara women visit the well. The embroidered tail protects the back of the head from the sun and the free end covers the pot. All is decorated with cowrie shells which are a sign of wealth, while three cowrie shell tassels hang from the lower edge.

410 x 230mm (16¼ x 9in)
Madhya Pradesh, North-west India, 1975–1980

272

right The Buyi village women from Anshun County wear these tassels, embroidered in silks with geometric diaper patterns, attached to their belts. Fine metal chains support the silk-wrapped 'God's Eye' pattern tassel heads, while silk-thread hanks, folded in half and tied with a knot, form the long tassels.

260 x 55mm (10¼ x 2⅛in)
South-west China, *c.* 1980

273

far left Little tassels are held with beads onto the punch stitch embroidered panels of a woman's festive over skirt from Guizhou Province. Silk tassel heads are decorated with stitches woven over and under a series of threads.

Detail 155 x 115mm (6¼ x 4½in)
South-west China, *c.* 1985

left A decorative version of a scholar's cap is worn by young girls in the Kunming area of Yunnan Province. Herringbone stitches and applied braids outline the curves of the cap, while the square of cross stitch embroidery that forms the top is bordered with a deep fringe of double loops in red synthetic threads.

180mm sq. (7in sq.)
South-west China, 1980–1985

275

above Feather and thread tassels alternate with little strings of Job's Tear seeds on the base of this hill-tribe shoulder bag. Buttons, seeds and metal discs decorate the embroidered surface. The seeds, which come from a tropical grass, are boiled to remove the pith. The feather tassels are woven on a bow loom, using a method similar to making rope handles for church bells.

350 x 260mm (13¾ x 10¼in)
North-west Thailand, *c.* 1980–1990

left A cluster of pompoms decorate the large and small 'God's Eye' shapes which are made from interlaced threads. These traditional hangings from Thailand can decorate the Temples, but smaller versions were used as courtship tokens. The maidens would throw them from their balconies and any young man who caught one could start courting the girl who made it.

230mm (9in)
North-west Thailand, *c.* 1990

right Although Tamari balls are popular in the West, they originally come from Japan and vary in size from large to very small. The pattern threads are wound round the ball in a pre-determined sequence, temporarily held by pins until the final round is in place. A silk thread tassel is added as a finishing touch to decorate suspended balls.

Diameter 50mm (2in)
Japan, *c.* 1995

277

right The lacy effect of little flower wheels
cascading from the pointed folds of this machine-
embroidered bag is achieved by working onto cold
water soluble fabric. The design is machined freely
so that all stitched lines interconnect to create a
stable, but gauzy, construction when the soluble
fabric is dissolved away. The wheels and rings are
worked on a flower stitcher device before
combining for the fringe.

584 x 165mm (23 x 6½in)
England, 2003
(Sandra Coleridge)

left Dyed organza fabric, stiffened with water-soluble fabric, has been used to make the organic plant shapes on this hanging tassel. The edges of the twisted shapes are supported with an outline of wire, machined in place, with added machine embroidery within the shapes. A partial dissolving of the soluble fabric gives firmness and support to the construction, which will revolve when suspended in the air.

152 x 533mm (6 x 21in)
England, 2002
(Penny Usher)

left The design elements of this contemporary wall hanging are repeated in the shapes of the tassels, so that they are an extension of the embroidery rather than just an addition. Stuffed and machine-embroidered heart shapes are complemented by the choice of decorative metallic beads threaded onto the strings that support the tassels.

127 x 508mm (5 x 20in)
England, 2002
(Ruby Lever)

left A variety of embroidery and textile techniques are used for a sampler of fabric edges, which becomes a decorative, finished piece in its own right. Edges are cut and lapped, bordered with fabric paint, folded under to become prairie points, even cut and rolled to make threaded fabric tabs. The triangle and diamond theme is carried into embroidery with looped stitches, machine embroidery, couched cords and fraying.

178 x 228mm (7 x 9in)
England, 2000
(Ruby Lever)

Chapter Eleven
Whitework

below Threads are withdrawn on a hand-woven, linen fabric to form a grid of squares that are then filled with needlelace stitches. The finished band would decorate bed linen or a cloth. This type of embroidery was the forerunner of free needlelace, but was adapted over the years to become linen cutwork embroidery, very popular in the late 19th century.

50 x 280mm (2 x 11in)
England, early 17th century

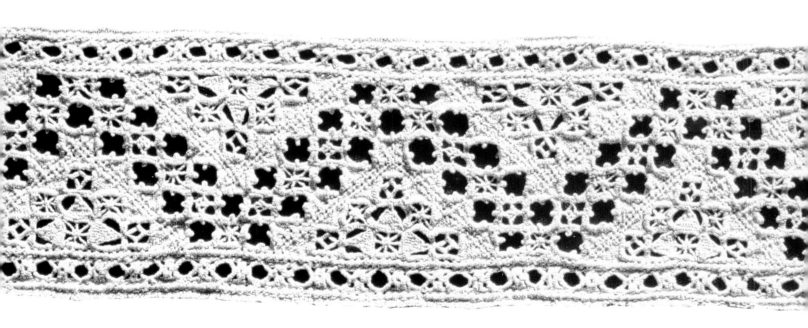

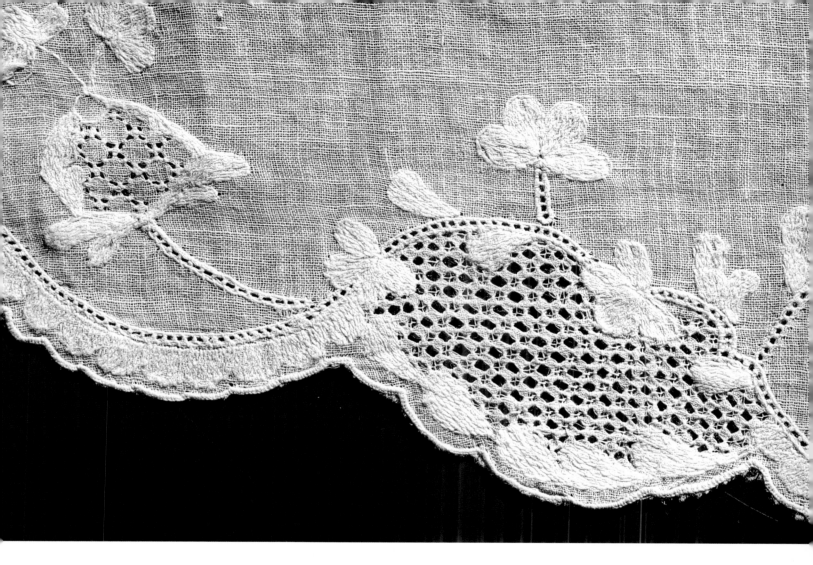

above The border of a dress sleeve ruffle is
embroidered to resemble the delicate lace
fashionable in the 18th century. Darning stitches,
worked in a soft linen thread, outline the pattern
motifs which contain a variety of pulled work
fillings. Close buttonhole stitching defines the
scalloped edge. Embroidery on fines linen fabric
may have originated in Saxony and is referred to
as Dresden work.

Detail 100 x 80mm (4 x 3⅛in)
Dresden, Germany, *c.* 1760–1780

left A fragment of fine cotton muslin cloth is the basis for white stitchery and cutwork of the highest order. Roses with buds and leaf sprays form the corner design, possibly for a stole. The fine scale stitches include padded satin, stem, speckled fillings and woven needlework fillings in the flower centres.

310 x 240mm (12½ x 9½in)
France, *c.* 1820–1825

Ayrshire Sewn Muslin and Broderie Anglaise

right A broad cape collar in Ayrshire sewn muslin would be worn over a dress with the very wide puffed sleeves fashionable in the late 1820s. The industry was set up by Mrs Jameison, the wife of an Ayrshire cotton merchant. She copied the floral designs from a French baby robe and her cottage outworkers became known as the Flowerers. A neat darn proves this collar was a treasured item.

225–445 x 74mm (9–17½ x 29¼in)
Ayrshire, Scotland, *c.* 1830

left A flowing design of fern fronds, leaves and flower buds scrolls across the broad surface. A variety of drawn thread patterns are worked into the medallion shapes, while padded satin stitch and couched trails delineate the fronds and leaf veins.

Detail 33 x 25mm (1¼ x 1in)
Ayrshire, Scotland, *c.* 1830

287

below and left This Ayrshire sewn muslin collar
was professionally made in the west of Scotland.
The embroidered collar would probably be worn
for best over a high-necked plain dress and took
the place of the more expensive lace collars.
Close examination of the collar shows the heavily
padded satin stitches, the couched trails that form
the ferns and drawn thread fillings within the
shield shapes. Close buttonhole stitches outline
the pointed scallops.

100 x 400mm (4 x 15⅜in)
Ayrshire, Scotland, *c.* 1835
(Anne Bate)

above The Ayrshire sewn muslin industry spread
across the sea to Northern Ireland. This baby
robe belonged to an Irish family and shows the
embroidered V-shaped top, bordered with frills
called robings. The triangle point overlaps a slit
in the waistband, and tradition demands that it
is tucked in for a girl and worn outside for a boy.

280 x 230mm (11 x 9in)
Northern Ireland, *c.* 1840–1845

right The design on the christening robe bodice shows the introduction of overcast eyelets, which at this date are worked together with the traditional Ayrshire stitches of stem, padded satin, drawn thread work and needlelace fillings.

Detail 115 x 50mm (4½ x 2in)
Northern Ireland, *c.* 1840–1845

above This baby robe bodice in Ayrshire-type stitchery includes a greater proportion of eyelet work, which was fast gaining in popularity, as it took slightly less time to do. The robings are bordered with parallel eyelet lines and decorated with buttonhole scalloped frills, as are the little sleeves. The skirt is missing, possibly remade into another garment.

310 x 190mm (12½ x 7½in)
England or Scotland, *c.* 1850

right A detail of the upper bodice shows the scrolling leaf designs together with a central rose which has a needlelace filling. By this date, the drawn thread fillings are seldom used. Padded satin stitch forms the flower petals, while couched trails are used for the stems.

Detail 40mm sq. (1½in sq.)
England or Scotland, *c.* 1850

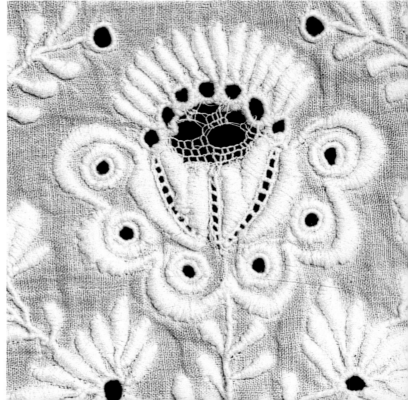

above A pattern of broderie anglaise or eyelet work stitch is used to decorate the front of this baby robe, made for a christening in 1862. The V-shaped insert on the front bodice is edged with broderie anglaise borders, called robings. The slotted waistband would be threaded with ribbon.

190 x 240mm (7½ x 9½in)
England, 1862
(Jane Bate)

293

left The skirt of the christening robe has a repeat of the grid pattern used for the bodice. This time the V-shape is inverted, while rows of eyelet stitchery follow the scalloped hemline. Eyelets are first outlined with a running stitch, slit both ways within the stitching, the surplus fabric is turned under and overcast stitches are sewn all round.

Detail 390 x 270mm (15¼ x 10½in)
England, 1862
(Jane Bate)

right An undersleeve or engageante was worn under the wide pagoda sleeves that were fashionable when the crinoline skirt reached its greatest width during the 1860s.

200 x 360mm (8 x 14¼in)
England, *c.* 1865
(Jane Bate)

Hedebo Embroidery

below Hedebo, meaning from the heath, is the
name given to Danish white embroidery worked
as part of a rural tradition onto the flat collars of
the men's shirts. Homespun linen was used as a
basis for satin, leaf and chain stitches which
outlined the overcast drawn work motifs. Bands
of needle-weaving are another feature of these
heavily embroidered collars.

400 x 190mm (15¾ x 7½in)
Denmark, *c.* 1790

top A border for a petticoat frill is worked
in a later, third form of the Danish Hedebo
embroidery. The cutwork areas have expanded
to include needlelace fillings and stitches now
include padded satin, buttonhole scallops and
overcast eyelets.

110 x 1930mm (4¼ x 76in)
England or Denmark, *c.* 1850

bottom The Italian influence of Venetian cutwork
patterns on the Hedebo designs soon increased the
areas of open work. A strip of cotton fabric has
most of the background cut away, leaving whipped
bars and satin stitch to hold the fabric together.
Machine lace is added to this border.

80 x 1930mm (3¼ x 76in)
England, *c.* 1870

above A section of unfinished tablecloth shows Hedebo embroidery in progress. Stitches include chain, Hedebo buttonhole, threaded herringbone, needlelace and needle weave fillings. An undulating border encases cutout areas for Hedebo motifs. The stamped pattern includes the trademark Penelope Copenhagen Design, Hedebo Reg.

Detail 340 x 225mm (13½ x 9in)
England, 1920
(*Ada Pearson*)

Mountmellick Embroidery

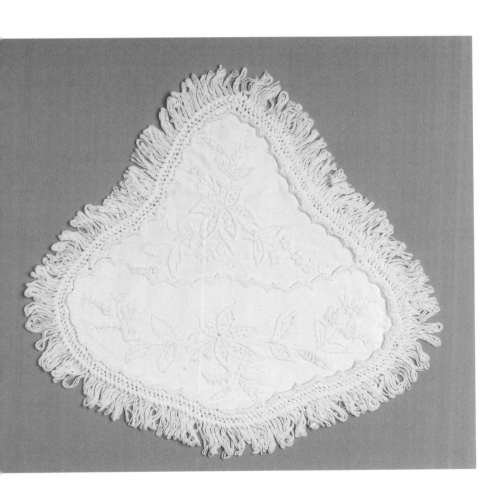

left Irish Mountmellick embroidery was introduced by Joanna Carter in 1825 to provide work after potato famines ravaged the country. Made to hang above a bed, a man's watch was popped into this pocket at night. Buttonhole scallops outline the pocket border, while flower and leaf sprays are worked in satin and stem stitches, twisted cable and rosette chain, French and bullion knots.

270 x 250mm (10½ x 9¾in)
Mountmellick, Ireland, *c*. 1850–1860

above A monogram letter B is sewn in fine cross stitch into the top corner of this little bag. The Mountmellick embroidery is worked onto a strong, twill weave cotton fabric. Cable plait stitch is used throughout to depict the central rose and leaf spray and the scrolling vines that form the borders. The drawstring has been replaced.

140 x 160mm (5½ x 6¼in)
Mountmellick, Ireland, *c.* 1870

above and right A Mountmellick revival in 1880 once again employed local women who embroidered domestic articles onto firm cotton fabric, using raised stiches to depict naturalistic designs. The central area shows flower and leaf motifs with trailing stems and spirals. Stitches include padded satin, feather, cable and twisted chain, braid stitch and long bullion knots. A knitted fringe in white cotton is the usual way of finishing Mountmellick work. This pretty, decorative pillow sham was used as a cover during the daytime.

510 x 370mm (20 x 14½in)
Mountmellick, Ireland, *c.* 1880

301

above Tape laces were very popular in the late 19th and early 20th century. A narrow, machine-made braid is tacked onto a pattern printed onto stiffened calico. Needlelace filling stitches are worked within the braid loops which are joined with wrapped thread bars. The tacking threads are cut to release the finished lace. Woven spiderweb wheels are a feature of this pair of little cuffs.

Detail 75 x 125mm (3 x 5in)
England, *c.* 1900–1910

left A tablecloth made as a wedding gift has white cotton fabric circles joined by crochet borders and insets. The rose and flower spreay is worked in padded satin stitch and back stitch. Buttonhole stitch outlines the leaves and flower petals and is used for the joining bars, while pulled thread work stitches decorate sections of the leaf motifs.

Detail 100 x 155mm (4 x 6⅛in)
England, 1951
(Gabrielle Whitehead Collection)

303

left The soft, painted petals of *Moon Daisy* float across a background made from deckchair fabric. Traditional Broderie Anglaise techniques form the flower centre with eyelet holes bound with hand-worked satin stitch. Stranded embroidery threads, Gutermann button thread and machine embroidery threads have been used, together with fabric paint to create this evening flower.

500mm sq. (19⅝in sq.)
England, 2004
(Nicola Jarvis)

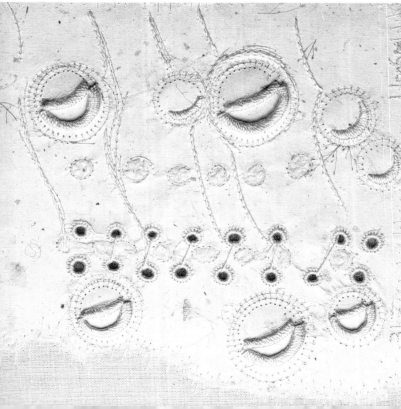

left Dyed and textured watercolour paper was chosen as the background for a design entitled *Urchin*, painted with gouache. Both machine-stitched lines and padded satin stitch are used to form the eyelets and cut-work shapes of historic whitework, translated into a modern design.

150–180mm sq. (6–7in sq.)
England, 2003
(Nicola Jarvis and Tracy Franklin)

above Manipulated fabrics and couched threads
are combined to give a three-dimensional effect to
the fan vaulting shown in this architectural detail.

300 x 210mm (11¾ x 8¼in)
Spain, 2004
(Milagros Martin)

above The cut-out spaces of historic Richleau
embroidery are chosen to make the petal shapes of
'Common Daisies'. Couched petal outlines are
held at intervals with vintage glass beads. A linen
fabric makes a background for fine chiffon and
strips of plastic carrier bags.

300 x 400mm (11¾ x 15¾in)
England, 2004
(Nicola Jarvis)

305

ACKNOWLEDGEMENTS

My first debt of gratitude is to my ancestors, whose expertise, enthusiasm and care for embroidery, patchwork and quilting was passed to me, both through the genes and as actual textiles which formed the basis of my collection. I would also like to thank all those friends and relations who have given items to add to those I already have, as well as to dealers in textiles and all the people in distant lands across the world who have made their embroidery available and given gladly of their time and knowledge.

Thanks are due to my immediate family, to my daughter, Jane Davies, for allowing me to use her City and Guilds and Art Foundation Course samples and to my son, Timothy Thompson, for his patient advice on photography, computer technology and help in setting up a comprehensive textile database. Thanks also to my grandson Christopher and daughter Jane for modelling the family smocks, and to my son and daughter for their gifts of foreign textiles and continuing support and interest in my endeavours.

I am very grateful to Marie Roper, City and Guilds tutor at Westhope College, Craven Arms, for allowing me to include her patchwork and quilting, as well as the work of her students, Catherine Craig, Bronwen Jenkins and Dorothy Symmonds, who gladly loaned their quilting and machine embroidery pieces for photography. To Lorna Pound of the Teme Valley Branch of the Embroiderers' Guild for permission to include her Dicken's Jack-in-a-Box and Afghan box creations. Alongside Margaret Hamer's work, this has allowed me to include City and Guilds Embroidery and examination work from different periods – from the 1940's to the beginning of the 21st century.

Many thanks to Jane Lemon, for allowing us to reprint her altar frontal and bead work cross, which first appeared in *Embroidery with Beads*, written for Batsford in 1987. Also to Sandra Coleridge, Ruby Lever, Sandra Meech, Penny Usher, Tracy Franklin, Nicola Jarvis and Milagros Martin, who allowed us to include their recently published work.

Thanks are due also to the Decorative Arts Museum, Tashkent, the Embroiderers' Guild, the Nottingham Museum of Costume and Textiles, Worcestershire County Museum and to Diana Banks, Gaynor Davies, Pat Scott and Gabrielle Whitehead for allowing me to photograph items from their collections. Thanks too, to the makers and designers of greetings cards and small pictures purchased some years ago, for whom I do not have current contact addresses.

I would like to thank my sister, Mary Liebemann and niece Anne for their textile gifts from South Africa, Mrs Bush and family for the Irish Christening robe, Kenneth Barham for the Chinese embroidered sachet, Eileen Dixson for the child's smock (page 256), Sylvia Fenwick for the Masai necklace and the gold embroidered cloth from Madras, Margaret Greene for the Chinese gold embroidered sleeve band, Pauline Milnes for the red Russian apron and the Anglo-Indian Coth (page 103), Jean Robson for the machine-embroidered cape, Pat Scott for the Indian Peacock purse, Margaret Storer for the unfinished Hedebo cloth, Kathleen Waller for allowing me to include the work given to me by her late sister, Margaret Hamer, and Winifred Womersley for the courthouse steps cot quilt.

Lastly, I would like to thank those who photographed and took such care of my textiles and all whose time and patience made this book possible.

Angela Thompson 2005

BIBLIOGRAPHY

Some of the books included in this list are old favourites, now out of print but obtainable from libraries on request. These books are invaluable for an understanding of the historical context. A selection of more recent books will give the embroiderer and quilter a modern perspective on new methods and design interpretations.

Countries

Africa
Sleigh, Mary, *African Inspirations in Embroidery*, BT Batsford, 2004
  (ISBN 0 7134 8921 9)
Stone, Caroline, *The Embroideries of North Africa*, Longman Group Ltd., 1985
  (ISBN 0 5827 8371 2)

China and Japan
Bertin-Guest, Josiane, *Chinese Embroidery, Traditional Techniques*, BT Batsford, 2003
  (ISBN 0 7134 8779 8)
Chatterton, Jocelyn, *Chinese Silks and Sewing Tools*, Jocelyn Chatterton, 2002
  (ISBN 0 9542173 0 6)
Chung, Young Yang, *The Art of Oriental Embroidery*, Bell and Hyman, London, 1979
  (ISBN 0 6841 6248 2)
Corrigan, Gina, *Miao Textiles from China*, The British Museum Press, 2001
  (ISBN 0 7141 2742 6)
Garrett, Valery M, *Mandarin Squares*, Oxford University Press, 1990
  (ISBN 0 1958 5239 7)
Gray, Julia D, *Beginner's Guide to Traditional Japanese Embroidery*, Search Press, 2001
  (ISBN 0 8553 2857 6)
Tamura, Shuji, *The Techniques of Japanese Embroidery*, BT Batsford, 1998
  (ISBN 0 7134 7991 4)

England

Johnson, Pauline, *Three Hundred Years of Embroidery 1600–1900*, Wakefield Press, 1986 (ISBN 0 9492 6881 X)

Kendrick, A F, *English Needlework*, A & C Black 1933 and 1967 (ISBN 0 7136 0164 7)

India and Pakistan

Gillow, John and Barnard, Nicholas, *Traditional Indian Textiles*, Thames and Hudson, 1993 (ISBN 0 5002 7709 5)

Yacopino Feliccia, *Threadlines Pakistan*, Ministry of Industries, Government of Pakistan, 1977

Myanmar (Burma)

Stanislaw, Mary Anne, *Kalagas: The Wall Hangings of South East Asia*, Ainslies, California, 1987 (ISBN 0 9618 4450 7)

Thailand

Lewis, Paul and Elaine, *People's of the Golden Triangle*, Thames and Hudson, 1984 (ISBN 0 5009 7314 8)

Turkey and Greece

Johnson, Pauline, *A Guide to Greek Island Embroidery*, Victoria & Albert Museum, 1972 (ISBN 0 9052 0913 3)

Johnson Pauline, *Turkish Embroidery*, Victoria & Albert Museum, 1985 (ISBN 0 9481 0702 2)

Taylor, Roderick, *Embroidery of the Greek Islands and Epirus*, Interlink Books, 1998 (ISBN 1 5665 6289 9)

Worldwide

Benn, Elizabeth (Editor), *Treasures from the Embroiderers' Guild Collection*, David and Charles, 1991 (ISBN 0 7153 9829 6)

Gillow, John and Sentance, Bryan, *World Textiles: A Visual Guide to Traditional Techniques*, Thames and Hudson, 1999 (ISBN 0 5000 1950 9)

Gostelow, Mary, *Embroidery: Traditional Designs, Techniques and Patterns from all over the World*, Marshall Cavendish Editions, 1977 (ISBN 0 8568 5236 8)

Ohms, Margaret, *Ethnic Embroidery*, Dryad, 1989 (ISBN 0 8521 9739 X)

Paine, Sheila, *Embroidered Textiles: Traditional Patterns from Five Continents*, Thames and Hudson, 1995 (ISBN 0 5002 7823 7)

Singer, Margo and Spyrou, Mary, *Textile Artists, Multicultural Traditions*, A & C Black, 1989 (ISBN 0 7136 3197 X)

Embroidery, Patchwork and Quilting

Appliqué

Puls, Herta, *The Art of Cutwork and Appliqué: Historic, Modern and Kuna Indian*, BT Batsford, 1978 (ISBN 0 7134 0476 0)

Beadwork

Andrews, Carol, *Making Needlework Accessories Embroidered with Beads*, Ruth Bean 2004 (ISBN 0 9035 8533 2)

Crabtree, Caroline and Stallebrass, Pam, *Beadwork, a World Guide*, Thames and Husdson, 2002 (ISBN 0 5005 1080 6)

Thompson, Angela, *Embroidery with Beads*, BT Batsford, 1987 (ISBN 0 7134 5495 4)

Embroidery

Campbell, Etta, *Linen Embroidery*, BT Batsford, 1990 (ISBN 0 7134 6251 5)

Eaton, Jan and Mundle, Liz, *Cross Stitch and Sampler Book*, Quill Publishing Ltd, 1985 (ISBN 1 8507 6012 8)

Geddes, Elisabeth and McNeill, Moyra, *Blackwork Embroidery*, Dover Publications, 1976 (ISBN 0 4862 3245 X)

Gostelow, Mary, *Blackwork*, BT Batsford, 1985 (ISBN 0 7134 4621 8)

Proctor, Molly G, *Victorian Canvas Work: Berlin Wool Work*, BT Batsford, 1972 (ISBN 0 7134 2647 0)

Swift, Gay, *The Batsford Encyclopedia of Embroidery Techniques*, BT Batsford, 1984 (ISBN 0 7134 3932 7)

Wark, Edna, *Drawn Fabric Embroidery*, BT Batsford, 1979 (ISBN 0 7134 1476 6)

Goldwork and Metal Thread Embroidery

Beese, Pat, *Embroidery for the Church*, Studio Vista 1975 (ISBN 0 2897 0531 2)

Dawson, Barbara, *Metal Thread Embroidery*, BT Batsford 1976 (ISBN 0 7134 3144 X)

Dean, Beryl, *Embroidery in Religion and Ceremonial*, BT Batsford, 1986 (ISBN 0 7134 5280 3)

Pyman, Kit, (Editor), *Gold and Silver Embroidery*, Search Press, 1987 (ISBN 0 85532 550 X)

Wark, Edna, *Metal Thread Embroidery*, Kangaroo Press, 1989 (ISBN 0 86417 242 7)

Machine Embroidery

McNeill, Moyra, *Machine Embroidery, Lace and See-through Techniques*, BT Batsford, 1985 (ISBN 0 7134 4485 1)

Machine Embroidery Trade Machines

Johnson, Beryl, *Advanced Embroidery Techniques*, BT Batsford, 1983
(ISBN 0 7134 0085 4)

Risley, Christine, *Machine Embroidery*, Studio Vista, 1973 (ISBN 0 2897 0098 1)

Patchwork and Quilting

Bishop, Robert, and Safanda, Elizabeth, *Amish Quilts*, first published by EP Dutton,
1976, new edition published by Laurence King, 1991 (ISBN 1 8566 9012 1)

Colby, Avril, *Patchwork*, BT Batsford, 1958 (ISBN 0 7134 5770 8)

Colby, Avril, *Quilting*, BT Batsford, 1972 (ISBN 0 1734 2645 4)

Meech, Sandra, *Contemporary Quilts: Design, Surface and Stitch*, BT Batsford, 2003
(ISBN 0 7134 8856 5)

Mende, Kazuko and Morishige, Reiko, *Sashiko, Blue and White Quilt Art of Japan*,
Shufunotomo Co. Ltd., 1991 (ISBN 0 87040 828 3)

Parry, Linda, (Editor) *A Practical Guide to Patchwork from the Victoria and Albert
Museum*, HarperCollins, 1987 (ISBN 0 0444 0050 0)

Rae, Janet, *The Quilts of the British Isles*, Constable, 1987 (ISBN 0 0946 8030 2)

Smocking

Andrew, Anne, *Smocking*, Murdoch Books, 1989 (ISBN 1 85391 060 0)

Bakewell, Ann-Marie, *Surface Embroidery and Smocking*, Lothian, 1993
(ISBN 0 85091 582 1)

Marshall, Beverley, *Smocks and Smocking*, Alphabooks, 1980 (ISBN 0 9506171 1 3)

Stitch Books

Butler, Anne, *The Batsford Encyclopedia of Embroidery Stitches*, BT Batsford, 1979
(ISBN 0 7134 3317 5)

Thomas, Mary and Eaton, Jan (Editor) *Mary Thomas' Dictionary of Embroidery Stitches*, first published 1934, new edition published by Caxton Editions, 2001 (ISBN 1860193129)

Tassels
Welch, Nancy, *Tassels: The Fanciful Embellishment*, Lark Books, 1992 (ISBN 0 937274 53 4)

Whitework
Bishop, Christine, *Schwalm Embroidery, Techniques and Designs*, Milner Craft Series, 1999 (ISBN 1 86351 220 9)

Bryson, Agnes F, *Ayrshire Needlework*, BT Batsford, 1989 (ISBN 0 7134 5928 X)

Dawson, Barbara, *Whitework Embroidery*, BT Batsford, 1987 (ISBN 0 1374 3590 5)

Houston-Almqvist, Jane, *Mountmellick Work: Irish White Embroidery*, Collin Smythe, 1985 (ISBN 0 85105 429 3)

Mitrofanis, Effie, *Casalguidi Style Linen Embroidery*, Kangaroo Press, 1997 (ISBN 0 86417 755 0)

Swain, Margaret, *Ayrshire and other Whitework,* Shire Album 88, Shire Publications, 1985 (ISBN 0 85263 589 3)

Swain, Margaret, *Scottish Embroidery: Mediaeval to Modern*, BT Batsford, 1986 (ISBN 0 7134 4638 2)

INDEX